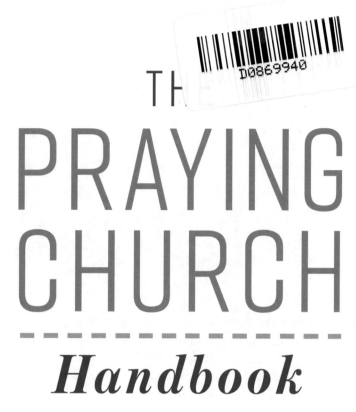

THE PRAYING CHURCH

Handbook

Ideas, Principles, and Guides for Local Church Prayer

COMPILED AND EDITED BY CAROL MADISON

PrayerShop PUBLISHING

TERRE HAUTE, IN

PrayerShop Publishing is the publishing arm of the Church Prayer Leaders Network. The Church Prayer Leaders Network exists to equip and inspire local churches and their prayer leaders in their desire to disciple their people in prayer and to become a "house of prayer for all nations." Its online store, prayershop.org, has more than 150 prayer resources available for purchase or download.

ISBN: 978-1-970176-02-5

1 2 3 4 5 | 2021 2022 2023 2024 2025

CONTENTS

FOREWORD

A number of years ago, I led a Christian publishing ministry that offered an optional prayer time for staff. We got together once a week to pray primarily for the ministry. Of course, we also touched on special personal needs if people requested prayer, but it was mostly about covering the Kingdom issues of the ministry.

We had a young staff member who was a fairly new believer. Sue (not her real name) came faithfully, every single week. But she never prayed out loud—until about two years into our prayer times. One morning, out of the blue, Sue offered up a two-sentence prayer. Her voice was shaky. She was clearly nervous. The next week she prayed again, this time with more confidence. And from there she was off to the races with prayer.

Today—25 years later—Sue is a seasoned, world-changing intercessor who prays bold, powerful prayers that force back the kingdom of darkness.

There are Sues in every church. In your church. We just need to find them, encourage them, equip them, and give them opportunities to pray.

That is what *The Praying Church Handbook*—and *Prayer Connect* magazine, where these chapters originally appeared—is all about. This book, compiled by Carol Madison, editor of *Prayer Connect,* is designed to give prayer leaders ideas and practical help in growing prayer in their churches.

The chapters of *The Praying Church Handbook* are written by seasoned, in-the-trenches prayer leaders. They understand prayer. They have experienced firsthand trying to grow prayer in a church. They understand the difficulties that come with being a pastor or prayer leader who is trying to equip, motivate, and mobilize a congregation to pray.

Their experience can make it easier for you as you lead your church into deeper levels of prayer. I encourage you to read through this book, then keep it close by where you can see it. You will open it again and again as you make plans for more prayer in your church.

I also encourage you, if you have not yet done so, to join the *Church Prayer Leaders Network* (see information in the back of this book). Why? Because its benefits, including *Prayer Connect,* will inspire, challenge, and equip you in your role of growing prayer with great ideas!

May God bless you as you seek to serve Him as a prayer catalyst in your local church.

—Jonathan Graf, President, Church Prayer Leaders Network

INTRODUCTION

As a prayer leader in my local church and editor of *Prayer Connect* magazine, I thrive on the ideas and experiences of other prayer leaders. One of my favorite meetings of the year—America's National Prayer Committee—happens every January in some warm climate. (As a Minnesotan, I appreciate the decision made by leaders years ago to never, ever hold the conference in a northern state!) I love sitting in the company of experienced prayer leaders from across the nation. They are devoted to mobilizing prayer around the country, ultimately with a view toward seeing churches established as "houses of prayer for all nations" (Mark 11:17). I drink lots of coffee, sit around tables with these prayer friends, and listen to fascinating stories and newly revealed prayer strategies to impact the local church and our entire nation.

I get to call these prayer leaders my friends. Over the years, I have gleaned much insight from those who lead, teach, and mobilize prayer. Many of the writers in this book received a personal invitation from me to write for the *Prayer Connect* magazine, based on their areas of expertise. As I've interacted with them and edited their articles over the years, I have matured into a better prayer leader.

This is our hope for you with this book. We have pulled some of the our best "Prayer Leader" columns and compiled them into *The Praying Church Handbook*. You now hold ideas, tips, tools, and inspiration from many of the most gifted prayer leaders in the nation.

And why is this so important for those of us who lead prayer ministries and try to inspire others? In this moment of history in our nation, a mobilized Church that prays with fervency and hope will invite the sweeping winds of revival and spiritual awakening. I can't think of a better way to invest my time!

–Carol Madison

ESTABLISHING YOUR CHURCH AS A HOUSE OF PRAYER

1

THE VOICE OF EXPERIENCE

By Jonathan Graf

P*rayer Connect* magazine asked seven national-level prayer leaders—individuals who regularly mentor and equip local prayer leaders—to answer this question:

> What is one thing you would like to say to local church prayer leaders to help them be more successful in their ministries?

Several leaders encourage prayer leaders not to give up or worry about small numbers. "Don't get discouraged," says Doug Small, liaison to the overseer for prayer for the Church of God (Cleveland, TN). "Go after a core of people."

Tom Swank, pastor and prayer leader in the Missionary Church, agrees. "Never give up! The stakes are incredibly high. There are too many lost people for us to abandon our prayer stations or cease to recruit others to join in praying the Lord of the harvest to send workers. . . . When it seems you are the only one praying, *never give up*. . . . When others don't understand your persistence in prayer, *don't give up*."

Check Your Own Heart

Phil Miglioratti and Alvin VanderGriend both emphasize that prayer is essential to the prayer leader's ministry. "Pray much and pray often for yourself," says VanderGriend, chairman of the Denominational Prayer Leaders Network. "[Ask] for the spiritual riches that God has for you in Christ—all the things He is eager to give to those who ask in accordance with His will" (1 John 5:14–15).

Miglioratti of the National Pastors Prayer Network emphasizes the vital importance of the Holy Spirit. "[There is] no better partner than the Holy Spirit to ensure a strong and successful ministry of prayer," he says. "The Spirit knows how to lead us, individually and corporately, in the *what*, *why*, and *how* of praying. So, next time you are praying or preparing or planning, or anything, invite the Spirit of the Lord to fill you (assume control, Eph. 5:18), to grant you the mind of Christ (1 Cor. 2:16), and to enable you to pray [as though seated] in the heavenly realms" (Eph. 2:6).

Expanding on the thought of praying for yourself as a prayer leader, Dennis Conner of Called to Serve, adds the idea of praying regularly "for the 'spirit of prayer' to fall upon the pastor, staff, and church leaders." This regular prayer pattern can change the spiritual dynamics of a church as God brings a vision for prayer to its leadership.

Recruit, Train, and Assist

Several other prayer leaders offer ideas to help recruit. "Ask God to call out a prayer team, with representation from the various areas of the church, to help draw members to participate in prayer opportunities," says Elaine Helms, the former national prayer director of the Southern Baptist Convention, now with Church Prayer Ministries. "When a member offers an idea for an avenue of prayer, ask how you may assist in getting that started. As you meet with the staff member regularly to encourage and equip him or her to lead that area of the ministry, you grow your prayer team naturally while mentoring a new leader."

Conner and David Chotka, a national prayer leader and pastor with the Christian and Missionary Alliance of Canada, both talked about the importance of teaching and training others. "Add a 4- or 6- to 8-week prayer training course that provides people the opportunity to do exactly what Jesus' first-century disciples wanted to do: learn to pray," comments Conner. "This practical step has made a huge difference in the churches that have done this. Their people become much more confident of how to pray more effectively. This course should be offered on a continual basis, so all the people have a chance to go through it."

Chotka, too, believes in the power of training, but he adds that you should start by using Jesus' plan—training those who can then train others. Jesus got alone with God; then He chose 12 to mentor, three of whom were especially close to Him. Encourage those you train to train others.

Prayer, Perseverance, and People

The bottom line: You simply cannot lead a prayer ministry if you are not convinced of the importance and power of prayer. Let your own prayer life demonstrate that you believe God's promise to hear the prayers of those who seek Him with humble hearts.

Then determine that you will not give up, regardless of the response to your invitations to pray. Persevere with the belief that one day God will demonstrate His answers to your heart cries.

And finally, always be thinking about bringing others along with you in this exciting prayer journey. Look for those you can mentor in prayer. Trust that the Lord will awaken His people to greater prayer if you are faithful as a leader.

JONATHAN GRAF is the president and founder of the Church Prayer Leaders Network and the publisher of *Prayer Connect* magazine.

EXPECTANT ATMOSPHERE OF A PRAYING CHURCH

- - - - - - - - -

By Thomas Swank

I love walking into a church where there is a sense of expectancy. Not expectancy of a great time of worship or inspiring teaching from God's Word, although both contribute to this atmosphere. What excites me is a sense of expectancy about what God is going to do and what He *is* doing.

I remember a church some years ago—not a large church—that was having a fruitful season. Each Sunday for weeks someone would respond to an invitation to receive Christ, or the church heard a report of someone surrendering to Christ during the week. A layman told me the congregation could hardly wait to go to church each week to see who had come to faith in Christ. They were faithfully bringing names of people before the Lord in prayer, and He was answering! The atmosphere was filled with expectancy.

A few years ago, a friend of mine led his church in a week of 24/7 prayer that was to conclude on Easter. After the Easter services, he left for vacation. When he returned, he was surprised to learn that the 24/7 prayer was continuing. It continued for more than two years with multiple answers to prayer and a growing expectation of what God was going to do. One young unbeliever accompanied a friend to the prayer room for her time to pray—and within the hour that unbeliever came to faith in Christ.

Early-Church Atmosphere

As you read the Book of Acts and the Epistles you soon feel the atmosphere of the early Church. Those early believers prayed with expectancy—and with confidence. Here are evidences of their confident practice of prayer:

- In all matters, prayer is the first priority rather than the last resort (Acts 2:42, 6:4).
- When opposition arises to the message of Christ, prayer is the spontaneous response (Acts 4:23–24).
- Prayer is an acknowledgement of faith in the Lord (Acts 4:24).
- Prayer focuses on the fulfillment of the great commission (Acts 4:29).
- There is a sense of expectancy in prayer (Acts 4:30).
- The presence and power of the Holy Spirit is evident (Acts 4:31).
- God's people are empowered to proclaim the good news (Acts 4:31, 33).
- The leaders are praying people, and they set an example of prayer for the congregation (Acts 1:14, 6:4).[1]
- Prayer is a way of life throughout the church. Not an isolated program, prayer permeates every ministry of the church (Eph. 6:18).[2]
- God's presence fills His house. Perhaps the single most distinguishing characteristic of a "house of prayer" is that it is filled with the tangible presence of God (Acts 2:2).
- With prayer, an increased spiritual hunger results in unbelievers coming to faith in Christ and believers deepening their faith (Acts 2).
- Spending time in the presence of the Lord produces humility, purity, unity, compassion, and Christlikeness in the lives of the leaders and the congregation (Col. 3:12).[3]

As we read about the practice of prayer in the early Church, we become aware of their conviction that "if God doesn't do this, it can't be done." They exhibit boldness born of desperation.

Recently a church layman told me about a property adjacent to his church that they had tried to purchase for years to expand their ministry. It was a residential property, but the owner was trying to get it rezoned commercial so he could ask a higher price. The church leadership called the church to prayer. Shortly after they began their concerted prayer, the owner sold them the property at less than the residential value.

Praying churches are confident that no matter what comes their way, God can handle it. Whether it is a changing neighborhood that threatens attendance, the death of a long-term pastor, or lack of clarity about future direction, a praying church has confidence, nurtured through the years, that God will lead them to continue expanding the Kingdom.

If prayer is not a priority, there will be no sense of expectation. Our focus disastrously shifts from expecting something from God to expecting the worship team to move us and the sermon to inspire us. We begin to look for what *we* can do rather than expecting what *God* might do.

Churches that consistently pray Kingdom prayers and celebrate answers will create an atmosphere of expectancy that produces confidence and boldness to ask God for great things.

[1]Cheryl Sacks, *The Prayer Saturated Church* (Colorado Springs: NavPress, 2007), 28.
[2]Ibid.
[3]Ibid.

THOMAS SWANK is director of PRAYFIRST!, the prayer ministry of the Missionary Church. He is a member of the Denominational Prayer Leaders Network.

INDICATORS OF A PRAYING CHURCH

- - - - - - - - -

By Carol Madison

I enjoy getting together once a month with a group of men and women who are just like me: they lead the prayer ministries in their churches and are eager to connect with others of like mind, heart, and assignment. We share resources, exchange ideas for prayer initiatives, and pray together. We try to stay apprised of the various local and national calls to prayer so that we might invite our congregations to participate.

Yet we are different in our emphases. Justin is particularly passionate about mentoring and mobilizing men in his church to pray with a worship focus. Valerie has developed an effective Drive-Thru prayer ministry in her community. Andrea oversees a ministry that helps people with healing kinds of prayer. I am especially engaged in mentoring a younger generation in prayer.

Whenever someone shares an idea or successful prayer initiative I think to myself, *Hey, we should do that.* Any of these prayer ideas and initiatives would enhance my church's prayer ministry. But as the director of prayer ministries, I have the responsibility of launching prayer initiatives that best fit our congregation—initiatives that God confirms He wants us to do.

Praying Church Indicators

So what does a praying church look like? Are there some common indicators that can help prayer leaders move in the right direction without trying to be like every other church?

A few years ago, I served on the Prayer First team, the denominational prayer ministry for Converge Worldwide. The team came up with a definition and description of a praying church that offers prayer leaders some general goals. With special thanks to Dana Olson (pastor of Faith Baptist Fellowship of Sioux Falls, SD), here is our definition: *A praying church is humbled, desperate, and hopeful in prayer, with a focus on worshiping Jesus Christ and praying Kingdom-minded prayers.*

We also developed a list of specific indicators of a praying church:

- A praying church is led by a praying pastor who has a heart to see the church become "a house of prayer for all people."
- A praying church encourages its members to establish personal and family prayer in their homes.
- A praying church establishes a "rhythm of prayer" on a weekly, monthly, quarterly, and yearly basis. Weekly and monthly prayer gatherings undergird the concerns and ministry needs of the church. A quarterly prayer gathering seeks to incorporate greater numbers of church members. A yearly prayer gathering may include praying with other like-minded churches for revival and evangelism.
- A praying church has a systematic way of praying for pastors and its leaders through the use of email or other prayer updates. This could include prayer teams designated for each staff member and elder, with a commitment to pray regularly for that leader.
- A praying church has a designated room or space as a "prayer room" that is resourced with helpful prayer tools. This prayer room can be used for prayer during services, special 24-hour seasons of prayer, small group prayer gatherings, or individual prayer times.
- A praying church offers regular prayer training opportunities to teach and model key prayer principles.

- A praying church recognizes intercessors who are especially gifted in prayer by identifying, equipping, and mobilizing them to pray in ways that acknowledge their unique gifting. It makes use of intercessors in strategic ways and develops prayer groups to encourage particular passions.
- A praying church makes effective use of social media and other communication to keep its members motivated and informed in prayer.
- A praying church engages in strategic prayer evangelism for the community, nation, and the world. This could include prayerwalking neighborhoods, adopting unreached people groups, praying for the nations, supporting missionaries in prayer—or any other way of praying toward the harvest.
- A praying church is connected to other national prayer initiatives.
- A praying church has a goal of motivating at least 50 percent of its congregation to some form of active prayer. It is a measurable prayer goal that is kept before pastoral staff.
- A praying church prays regularly for other churches and is willing to mentor and encourage them in prayer.

You may not hit every one of these points, but keeping these goals in mind can help you, as a prayer leader, to move your church closer to being identified as a praying church—as God is uniquely calling you.

CAROL MADISON is editor of *Prayer Connect* magazine and director of prayer ministries at Hillside Church of Bloomington, MN. She is the author of *Prayer That's Caught and Taught*, available at *prayershop.org*.

4

RESENTERS, RESISTERS, AND THE PRIDE DIVIDE

By Daniel Henderson

There was a time I believed every church member would automatically and wholeheartedly embrace the call to prayer. I have since learned otherwise.

The culprit that has spoiled my expectations is pride. I call it "the pride divide." Because the enemy is always counterattacking any renewed emphasis on prayer, the insipid infection of pride can infiltrate the hearts of both those who embrace the prayer initiatives and those who do not.

Scripture describes pride as the snare or trap of the devil (1 Tim. 3:7). The snare makes its way into the prayer movement so subtly that it is hardly noticeable until the symptoms show up in serious conflict.

Two camps can easily emerge in any church. The first group I call the "resenters" and the second, the "resisters." No one *plans* to join either camp, but the signs of subtle pride are obvious once they occur.

A Snare Emerges

Resenters can surface among those who jump wholeheartedly into the prayer ministry. As they relish their new experiences, they share the blessings of prayer with great enthusiasm. Prayer is something that must be experienced and can seldom be adequately explained, so others who aren't as involved may not share the excitement.

This lack of participation can be interpreted as a lack of spirituality—or a failure to support the leadership of the church. Soon the prayer-energized saints begin to resent the nonparticipants. Without great care and sensitivity, a pharisaical pride can surface.

As a response, the resisters—nonparticipants—begin to dig in their heels and even become antagonistic to the new initiatives. Typically, they are reacting more to the overbearing zeal of the enthusiasts than to the actual call to prayer. Pride unfortunately enters on both sides.

Deconstructing the Pride Divide

In my years of prayer leadership as a pastor, the following lessons have helped break down the pride divide, keeping everyone focused on the right goals:

1. Honesty is the best policy. Church leaders must acknowledge the divide, or at least the potential for it, and determine to address it openly with understanding and grace. Several times over the years, I have spoken openly from the pulpit on a Sunday morning about this dilemma. Just the act of exposing this danger allows people to talk about it, recognize it, and find greater resolve to avoid it. It also serves public notice on the forces of darkness that we are all alert to their schemes.

2. Understanding goes a long way. It is helpful for the resenters to remember that just because individuals cannot participate in the prayer programs does not mean they are less committed to seeking the Lord. The "holdouts" may have a variety of legitimate reasons for not participating in the call to united prayer.

Leaders would do well to explain to the resenters that public prayer activity is not the only gauge of spiritual authenticity. And resisters need reminders that the extreme outward zeal of the prayer adopters often reflects a sincere and seeking heart, for which we should always be grateful.

3. Prayer is intimacy, not activity. As prayer ministry develops, we can easily get wrapped up in the activity of prayer and lose focus on the core issue of relationship with God. This is the contrast we see between the prayer approach of the Pharisees and that of Jesus. In His Sermon on the Mount Jesus reprimanded the Pharisees for reducing prayer to a public display of religious superiority. In contrast, He told His followers to humbly gather in a secret place to experience intimacy with their Father in heaven (Matt. 6:1, 5–13). Similarly, we can fall into the trap of making prayer a "program for God" rather than the pure and simple pursuit of His person and presence.

4. Only the Holy Spirit can motivate people to pray. Ultimately, only the Holy Spirit can draw people into a deeper commitment to prayer. Jesus wants His Church to be a house of prayer, and His Spirit is able to make it so. Each of us must find his or her place in this plan, and graciously pray that others will do the same. In an environment of humility and grace the pride divide cannot thrive for long.

Grace for the Pride Divide

Real humility works in concert with honesty, understanding, intimacy with Christ, and a focus on the power of the Holy Spirit. Humility invites grace and allows us to express mutual submission. Resenters can trust Christ for the grace that will draw others into prayer. Resisters can receive the grace that will lead them into prayer.

Together they will be exalted to a higher level of spiritual understanding and intimacy as they learn to seek the Lord on the common ground of humility.

DANIEL HENDERSON is the president and founder of Strategic Renewal, a ministry that exists to ignite personal renewal, congregational revival, and leadership restoration (*strategicrenewal.com*).

AN ACTIVE PRAYER ROOM CAN FUEL YOUR CHURCH

- - - - - - - - -

By Esther Leonard

At Mountain View Church we believe the prayer room is the boiler room, the furnace, and the nuclear power plant of the church. Because of this, we keep it fueled and ready.

Naturally there are many questions about establishing a specific, designated room in your church for prayer. Why would a church have a prayer room? How big should it be? Who will maintain it? How creative does it need to be? How do we get people to use it?

The answers are harder to come up with than the questions. At our church we have addressed these questions and many others around the issue of prayer with one answer: "It's not our problem to solve. The prayer room is *one way* we encourage people to enter into God's most Holy Presence."

If our questions revolve around whether people are excited about it or how many are lining up to get in, then we will find ourselves discouraged. Just as we can't create revival, we can't create a prayer culture that all will embrace.

Creative and Ever-Changing Prayer Room

We are committed, however, to our church's passion to be a "house of prayer for all the nations." So let me offer a few suggestions for establishing a prayer room in your church:

1. Pray for people to receive a God-glorifying, Jesus-given, Holy Spirit-empowered passion to pray.
2. Put passionate service into your prayer room preparation even if you and a few prayer leaders are the only ones who will use it. Remember, we are doing this for God. It needs to be excellent and creative.
3. Throughout the course of a year, resources in the room should regularly change to track the sermons and follow national and international days of prayer. Resources should also focus on revival, evangelism, missions, etc. As your church changes, your prayer room should also change to match the emphases.
4. Be creative in setting up the prayer room. Recruit a team of people who will help resource it so there is variety and clear instruction on what to do when you enter the room. Encourage prayers of praise, prayers of repentance, prayers for the lost, missions, youth, preaching, Sunday services, the world, and finances. Be sure to include a children's section so they can come with their parents and not be bored.
5. Faithfully use the prayer room yourself and invite your staff, leadership, and ministry leaders to use it as well. Model your enthusiasm for making use of the room by inviting others to join you.
6. Preach about the power of the prayer room in Sunday messages and other teaching opportunities.
7. Offer prayer room "open houses" to give people tours and entry into a prayer experience. This means the room must be clean, organized, and always ready for guests—just like your home.
8. Communicate often that the prayer room is not only for the super-spiritual or those who are mature in their faith. It is crucial that intercessors be sensitive when speaking of "great joys and spiritual experiences" in the

prayer room. Avoid using prayer jargon that intimidates most people.

9. Use the prayer room only for personal prayer or specific prayer meetings. Try not to let it become a meeting room for various groups in the church. Instead, reserve it as a special place for individuals to pray at any time.

10. Have a sign-in book so you can track real numbers—not just what you *think* is happening. This will keep you encouraged and provide accountability to you, your staff, and leadership about the actual use of the room. People track what they value. Thus, if we value the prayer room, we will track its use.

11. Enjoy the room. Make it fun. God is not a hard, difficult Lord and Leader. It is fun to hang out with Him!

Prayer is not a ministry of the church that we delegate to a few or pass on to a select group. The priesthood of all believers is the center of everyone's life and calling. It is the intimate communication part of our relationship with God—connecting our lives and our hearts. We can never delegate this to an individual or a committee.

Each follower of Jesus is to have his or her own personal lifeline of communication with Jesus as our Leader, spending time each day interacting with our Savior. And the prayer room is one intentional way we are blessed to do this.

ESTHER LEONARD serves as prayer coordinator at Mountain View Community Church in Fresno, CA—a Mennonite Brethren Church that she and her husband Fred (lead pastor) founded in 1994.

DON'T FORGET YOUR OWN PRAYER LIFE!

By Douglas Kamstra

In the busyness of praying with people, leading prayer meetings, organizing prayer initiatives, developing new ministries, teaching on prayer, recruiting prayer warriors, and encouraging intercessors, it is easy to forget about one's own prayer life. Under the weight of leadership and the demands of ministry, our prayer life—nurturing our personal relationship with Jesus—is often the first thing we tend to neglect.

All too often when we talk about *prayer leaders*, we seem to have the order inverted. I've heard speakers recommend that when churches are looking for someone to build (or lead) the prayer ministry in their church, they should look for someone with leadership and teaching gifts rather than someone who spends hours each week on their knees.

But my question is, shouldn't we have both? Shouldn't *prayer leaders* also be fervent pray-ers? All too often we put the emphasis on being *leaders*, rather than on being *pray-ers*. The term *prayer leader* suggests, rightly so, that *prayer* should come first—before *leader*ship.

Resetting Priorities

My initiation into prayer ministry came when another prayer leader invited me to take a two-week intensive Spirituality and Ministry class at Fuller Seminary. We spent the intervening weekend in the desert, literally, at Saint Andrews—a Benedictine monastery. Challenged to enhance our prayer lives, we sat in the desert alone in silence—and in prayer. I'd never done that before. It reset my priorities.

All of the studies on prayer I've ever encountered indicate that the average Christ-follower spends about five-to-seven minutes a day in prayer. Pastors survey only slightly higher. I've never seen a survey of how much time *prayer leaders* spend in prayer, but I know well-trained and highly educated prayer leaders who are so busy mobilizing others to pray that their own prayer lives suffer. Periodically, I even see my own prayer life in that mirror.

Prayer leaders are busy people. Leading prayer ministries and mobilizing people to pray is an always challenging, sometimes frustrating, periodically exhausting, and usually underappreciated work. So sometimes we find ourselves speaking "out of our training" rather than out of our personal experience. Sometimes we realize we are leading out of our spiritual giftedness instead of an intimate relationship. While it may not *surprise* us that in many prayer meetings we spend more time talking about prayer than actually praying, it should *concern* us.

Jesus' Prayer Life

The public prayer life of Jesus was saturated with daily praying—from the *Shema* (a prayer of profession, Deut. 6:4–5) to the *Amidah* (a prayer of 18 benedictions) to the *Berakhot* (prayers of blessing throughout the day). Jesus was constantly praying with and teaching His disciples (and the crowd) throughout the day, but it wasn't enough. The Greatest Pray-er would get up "very early in the morning, while it was still dark . . . [and go] off to a solitary place" (lit. *eremos topos*; Mark 1:35)—to be alone with His Father.

In Galilee, just outside Capernaum, there is a place known as Prayer Mountain (i.e., Mount Arbel). Each day, rabbis (the *prayer leaders* of Jesus' day) would rise early and climb this rugged mountain for the sole purpose of being close to the Father. This was no small feat during the day and a considerable challenge in the moonlight. It required incredible effort, energy, and fortitude to make the trek each morning. But they (and Jesus) did so because they understood that extended time praying "in a solitary place" was not optional but, rather, an absolute necessity.

When we remember that at His incarnation Jesus *emptied* Himself (i.e., set aside His divine power and prerogative), we begin to realize it was Jesus' prayer life—His pursuit of intimacy with His Father from the beginning of His ministry (Mark 1:35), throughout His ministry (Mark 6:46), and until the very end of His ministry (Mark 14:32–42)—that empowered Him to teach, cast out demons, and heal the sick with authority (Mark 1:14, 25, 31).

Slow Down and Go Silent

All believers, but especially *prayer leaders*, must embrace the prayer life of Jesus. Pursue time with your first love (Rev. 2:4). You have *His* permission to slow down to nurture your heart and soul. Find a solitary place and spend 20–30 minutes in silence every day. As leaders we need to stay vigilant!

Spend some extended time with the Father—for adoration, confession, intercession, petition, and thanksgiving. But most of all, just be with Him, listen to His voice, and enjoy His company. It will transform your life. It will empower your ministry.

DOUGLAS KAMSTRA has been a prayer leader at the local, denominational, and national levels for more than 30 years. He is the chair of the Denominational Prayer Leaders Network and the author of *The Praying Church Idea Book* (available at *prayershop.org*). He is also a spiritual director, seminar speaker, and retreat leader.

LEADERSHIP AND PRAYER RELATIONSHIPS

7

WHEN PASTORS AND INTERCESSORS STRUGGLE

- - - - - - - - - -

By Phil Miglioratti

I've lost count of how many times an intercessor has spoken to me about the lack of interest or cooperation from his or her pastor in building a prayer culture throughout their congregation. And I have had too many conversations with pastors regarding the unpredictability of a prayer leader in a church.

These situations, no doubt, explain why "Let the Healing Begin" is the opening chapter of Eddie and Alice Smith's groundbreaking book, *Intercessors and Pastors: The Emerging Partnership of Watchmen and Gatekeepers.* They recognize that "the relationship of respect, effective communication, and meaningful partnership of the watchmen and the gatekeepers must be restored if the church is to regain her spiritual integrity, glorify Christ, and demolish the gates of hell" (p. 8).

More than a decade later, sadly, the work of restoring this crucial ministry relationship is far from complete. The following four realities continue to compromise upward-reaching, life-giving, forward-moving prayer in the Church.

Reality #1. Satan hates unity.

God's enemy knows that the unity of the Church powerfully demonstrates to lost people that God loves them and sent Jesus to show us His love (John 17:23). Satan is eager to steal our attention from prayer, kill the voice of the Spirit heard only in intercession, and destroy hope-filled praying (John 10:10). We play into the enemy's hands when we wrestle with our flesh-and-blood brothers and sisters in Christ (Eph. 6:12).

Reality #2. Some pastors are insecure.

Not every pastor is eager to break tradition or try new approaches to ministry. Some assume the ritual or routine they have learned is the only theologically correct way to speak with God. Others have a need to be in control. Delegating a ministry or relinquishing responsibility to another member of the Body is disconcerting, especially when it allows the Holy Spirit greater freedom in shaping the direction and style of praying across the congregation. And, sadly, some pastors have ineffective prayer lives and are therefore weak when it comes to leading church members into "upward-outward-forward" prayer.

Reality #3. Some intercessors are peculiar.

Peculiar is not a derogatory term; I use it to assert that many individuals—gifted or called into a ministry of intercession—have a personality very different from that of an organizational leader. They are attuned to times of quiet and introspection with high sensitivity to hearing from the Lord. This can intimidate a pastoral leader. Sadly, intercessors can confuse hearing from the Lord with having authority from the Lord to issue "prophecies" without submitting them to pastoral protocol. In these cases, it is easy to appear as if they fail to respect godly authority or they are eager to be in the spotlight.

Reality #4. Trust is a delicate thing.

Relationships require TLC (truthful, loving communication, Eph. 4:15). Making the pastor-intercessor relationship even more challenging is the reality that many intercessors are female and most pastors are male. Protecting the partnership with appropriate and safe boundaries can also create distance and hinder personal or intimate communication.

Working Toward a Better, Biblical Partnership

The Apostle Paul, in Philippians 4:2, provides a good start for working together effectively: "I entreat *and* advise Euodia and I entreat *and* advise Syntyche to agree *and* to work in harmony in the Lord" (AMP). Both names appear to be feminine, but the first half of each name is instructive: *euo* means "good"; *syn* means "together." Applying this principle also to pastors and intercessors, they are exhorted to agree, urged to work together because, as one translation says, "you belong to the Lord" (NLT).

Pastors need to remember their responsibility: "to prepare God's people for works of service, so that the body of Christ may be built up" (Eph. 4:12). Teaching people to pray and training those who are most gifted to lead meetings or ministries of prayer is a direct application of that instruction.

Intercessors need to remember that in many situations, their role is to be nearly invisible because humility is the primary component of a life God blesses. God opposes the prayers of the proud but responds graciously to humble pray-ers who seek to only lift Christ and not themselves (1 Peter 5:5).

We all need to remember the key role of the designated prayer leader. He or she has the opportunity to interpret the style and substance of the intercessor's messages to the pastor and to help the intercessor see that their pastor not only believes in prayer but values it in all phases of the congregation's ministry.

The Apostle Paul speaks to a pastor, Timothy, with an urgency to make prayer a priority (1 Tim. 2:1). It is incumbent upon every pastor, all intercessors, and each prayer leader to make sure nothing stands in the way—so that every person, every program, and every plan is birthed and bathed in prayer.

PHIL MIGLIORATTI is the curator and coordinator for The #ReimagineFORUM @ Pray. Network, a collaboration of prayer-fueled leaders who are applying Romans 12:2 ("don't be conformed; be transformed") to their understanding and their ministry of prayer.

8

RALLYING PRAYER SUPPORT FOR YOUR PASTOR

- - - - - - - - -

By Kaye Johns

Most churches have great intentions regarding prayer for their pastoral staff. But getting people to pray for their pastor(s) consistently is a bit more difficult. If you have a heart to pray for your pastor and a desire to identify and encourage others to pray as well, where do you start? Here is a simple plan:

1. Pray about it.

Ask God to lead you to others with a similar desire, and to prepare their hearts to want to join you. Pray about which individuals, specifically, to ask before you contact them. You will have more success in recruiting people who already have a heart to pray this way—and the Spirit will lead you to them.

2. Begin with a core group.

Don't worry about the numbers. Start with a small group of committed people. You'll want to name the group so it can be readily identified within the church. It's important to define the group with a stated purpose, simple guidelines, and expectations. You also want to be sure that the church leaders know about your group and are willing to endorse it.

3. Invite the people on your list to a start-up meeting.

Explain your heart for praying for the pastor and ask them to join you. Explain how you will be organized, generally, but ask for their input. Some things to consider:

- What is the purpose of your group? Your purpose will be to pray for your pastor, and, if you choose, for his or her family. Keep the purpose simple, clear, and focused. If you have a larger staff, you will need to decide if you are praying primarily for the senior pastor or for all the pastors.

- How long are you asking people to commit to pray? Having a specific time frame of three months, six months, or a year provides a way for people to make a realistic initial commitment.

- How will you communicate with the group? Email is one of the most efficient ways. Create an email contact group and email people on a regular basis to keep them informed and motivated.

- What will the group be expected to pray for? Some pastors may provide prayer requests, but in the beginning, it will be helpful to center the group's prayer around Scripture.

- How often are you asking them to commit to pray? Daily? Once a week? Be sure to include the words "at least" daily or once a week, or "as the Lord leads." You want to help people set realistic commitments they can succeed in keeping.

- After your initial meeting, send out revised guidelines based on your discussion to those who attended the meeting and others who may join your group later.

4. Support and encourage your group.

Once people have committed to pray, they will need your encouragement to stay on task over a period of time. Consider these things:

- What prayer resources will you provide? Perhaps the most important thing will be Scripture prayers or verses they can use as personal prayer prompts. When you come across other encouraging resources, be sure to share them.

- How often will you provide resources? Once a week you could send new verses or prayers. These can serve as weekly reminders to pray.
- Will you meet together periodically? Coming together will give you the opportunity to pray corporately and share prayer resources. As you conclude your first year, you might consider a more formal gathering, perhaps with the pastor. Use the occasion to thank people and provide the opportunity for them to reenlist.
- How will you keep your group committed? People need to be shown appreciation. Be intentional about affirming them on a regular basis with handwritten notes or emails. Pray for each one by name.

5. Encourage praying for the pastor throughout your church membership.

Offer regular invitations for new people to join your group.

- Visit small groups. Enlist the help of your primary prayer group to visit classes and Bible studies to encourage people to add your pastor to their group prayer lists and personal prayer times.
- Use the Sunday worship guide or church bulletin. Ask if you can include a weekly Scripture verse to pray for your pastor and other church leaders.

As prayer leaders in our churches, we can't motivate people to pray for our pastor. Only God can. Our role is to provide opportunity, resources, and encouragement for those whose hearts He touches.

KAYE JOHNS and her husband Jim founded PrayerPower Ministries in 1994. Their website (*prayerpowerministries.com*) offers prayer training and other practical materials.

PROTECTING PASTORS THROUGH STRATEGIC PRAYER

By Adena Hodges

In the 1990s, one of the regions in a very dark part of Kenya, Africa, was known as the graveyard of pastors and missionaries. It seemed that no work of God could be established there.

But a pastor with a team of intercessors was determined to see God's Kingdom advance. They tried many prayer and worship methods, but still experienced considerable opposition. Then, in desperation, the pastor asked each of his intercessors to take a day of the week to fast and pray for him and the ministry.

In the beginning, there was a measure of breakthrough. However, one by one, the intercessors were "picked off" through sickness or accidents. Realizing the vulnerability of the intercessors as they fasted and prayed for their leader, the pastor then asked two intercessors to also cover the intercessor who was praying for the pastor on his or her assigned day.

When they began to do this, breakthrough happened! Today, there are many churches in this region as well as a Bible college (source: compilation by Beni Johnson, *Prayer Changes Things*, chapter 9).

The Power of Strategy

This simple prayer strategy changed everything! It was not complex, but it produced a significant turnaround in the futile attempts to advance God's Kingdom.

Without strategy, battles are lost, businesses fail, and people walk aimlessly through life. We cannot afford to be isolated or alone on the battlefield of prayer. We must learn to come together, understand one another's gifts, callings, and assignments as we fight strategically side by side.

Picture intercessors similar to the military. There are different branches (Army, Marines, Navy, Air Force, Coast Guard) with specific roles and assignments. Each branch knows its part and function. Working together brings victory in war. As intercessors learn to appreciate each other's differences, operate in their strengths and pray strategically, we'll see much greater advances for the Kingdom of God.

Seal Teams in Prayer

While we need everyone to be engaged in prayer for churches, pastors and leaders, there can also be a specific type of prayer team that comes around the pastor—much like a "Seal Team" in the military. These team members have a special and strategic role in assisting the pastor in by providing additional spiritual coverage and protection.

Using the simple model from the example of the pastor and his intercessors in Kenya, my church implemented the idea of Seal Teams. The Seal Teams use strategy, communication, and unity. They not only fast and pray for the pastor, but they also cover each other in prayer. When it is one intercessor's turn to fast and pray for the pastor, the people assigned to the days before and after also pray for the intercessor.

Since implementing this model in our church in 2011, we've seen incredible breakthroughs. Whenever the pastor was struggling with discouragement before a service, he would text the team, and within minutes he would feel the weight of oppression lift and freedom to preach. Throughout that first year, it was amazing to see major obstacles removed and lives changed.

There were other benefits we hadn't anticipated with these teams. Too often there are breaches between pastors and intercessors that have long divided and decreased effectiveness in ministry. Often a pastor is willing to have intercessors who pray off in a corner or back room, but might have difficulty working directly with them. Through these special dedicated teams, bonds are formed between the pastor and the intercessors that produce abundant fruit.

In addition, a culture of prayer is developed as the teams learn to pray for one another. You can't pray for someone regularly without coming to love and appreciate him or her in new ways.

Prayer Points for Leaders

As you develop Seal Teams, it is helpful to have some common prayer points that encourage intercessors to pray in agreement. Here are some helpful prayer points:

1. Pray for strengthening the "inner man" of your pastor. Paul says in Ephesians 3:16, ". . . to be strengthened with might through His Spirit in the inner man" (NASB). Often we pray for outward things, but miss what's going on in the heart.

2. Pray for effective team leadership. Pastors were never meant to "go it alone," but this is often the model demonstrated. Ask the Lord to surround your pastor with trusted, faithful leaders and intercessors to help fulfill the calling on his or her life.

3. Pray for courageous pastors who will ask for help when needed. Most pastors feel they can't trust anyone with the battles and struggles they are going through. This isolates them and keeps them from sharing until sometimes too late.

4. Pray for seasons of rest. Pastoring is one of the most difficult jobs around. It's often 24/7 with little reward or compensation. Encour-

age your pastor to get away for times of rest and refreshment.

For more information and training, go to *intercessorsworkshop.com* or contact the author at *adena@EquippingTheKingdom.com*.

ADENA HODGES and her husband Gil are co-directors of the Kingdom Equipping Center in Roseville, CA (*equippingthekingdom.com*). She is also the author of two books and writes a weekly blog at *1000waystopray.com*.

ENHANCING CORPORATE PRAYER

10

LEARNING TO PRAY TOGETHER

By Douglas Kamstra

"**B**efore we leave, let's spend a few moments in prayer. . . ."

As a specialized transition pastor and denominational prayer leader, I've spent a lot of time in church meetings. It's encouraging that leaders are pausing to pray during these meetings; it's discouraging that for so many leaders, prayer is simply an add-on to their work and ministry.

"Bob, if you would begin, I'll finish after we've all prayed."

The opening pray-er provides the initial address to God, then passes the "baton" to his right. The next pray-er prays through his list of five or six requests. The third pray-er now mentally crosses off three of her items that the previous pray-er mentioned, and she mentions five more. Eight or nine minutes later, the seventh pray-er concludes the prayer.

"Amen."

"All right, everyone. Thanks for coming. See you next month!"

Changing the DNA

Prayer, as has often been said, is the work of the church. The correlation between praying churches and healthy growing churches has been proven. But the prayer level of a congregation seldom rises above the passion level in the prayers of its leadership.

We need to learn to pray. But, even more importantly, we need to learn to pray *together*. Most of the group praying I've observed is actually little more than a string of individual prayers spliced together.

Changing the DNA of prayer in our churches requires a great deal of fortitude and perseverance. The early Church learned how to pray together, and they set the world aflame with the gospel. Although some training and education are always helpful, little will change until we actually start praying *together*.

So, at the next church meeting, small group, or prayer group you attend, suggest and integrate one or two of the following (recognizing change takes time):

1. Pray together at the beginning of the meeting. "Praying first" underscores the importance of prayer and sets the context for the meeting. When prayer is relegated to the end of the meeting, participants are looking at their watches, focused on getting home. Set aside a block of 30 minutes minimum at the top of the agenda.

2. Begin with silence. Most of those in attendance have had busy days. People need some silence to reset their souls.

3. Remind everyone to pray throughout the entire prayer time. By encouraging participants to also pray silently and continuously, you remove the expectation that everyone pray aloud. Typically in group prayer, participants are only half listening to what others are praying because they are thinking about what they are going to pray when their turn comes.

Silence is always acceptable. It doesn't necessarily mean we can't think of anything else to pray for. Silence is an opportunity for the Spirit to work in our hearts.

4. Pray aloud only when prompted by the Spirit. When you feel the

Holy Spirit's encouragement, pray aloud. Focus on praying what you sense the Spirit is inviting you to pray. That is, pray God's agenda—often a continuation of what is currently being prayed.

5. Pray one praise, one confession, or one intercession at a time. Praying one item at a time allows others to participate in praying for that same need. When that need has been saturated with prayer, the Spirit will provide another praise, confession, or need for prayer.

6. Pray in agreement. When you pray aloud, you are articulating the Spirit-directed prayer on behalf of the community of Christ, so use plural pronouns: "*Our* Father . . . give *us our* daily bread, deliver *us* from evil. . . ."

7. Pray Scripture. When we pray Scripture, we are praying God's will. Praying Scripture assures us we are praying *together.*

8. Pray Kingdom prayers. The focus of many prayer gatherings is on *us*—our personal needs or items on our prayer list. Encourage broader prayers, such as prayers for the protection of believers, for unity among Christ-followers, for revival in the nation, for global evangelization, for growing awareness of God's presence. Kingdom prayers are prayers we can all pray *together.*

By beginning in prayer, you will lay the foundation to return to praying at any time and for any reason the Spirit might provide. "These all with one mind were continually devoting themselves to prayer. . ." (Acts 1:14, NASB).

DOUGLAS KAMSTRA is a specialized transition minister, spiritual director, leader of the *Deeper Journey* (a ministry to deepen intimacy with God through the spiritual disciplines), author of the *Praying Church Idea Book*, and chair of the Denominational Prayer Leaders Network.

ENCOURAGING RELUCTANT PRAY-ERS

By Daniel Henderson

One of our men recently wrote these words, "I wish my writing could reflect the passion and deep feelings I have experienced since I have become involved in the prayer ministry. My eyes have been opened and God has allowed me to see His world in a whole new way and to experience prayer to a much different level than I ever felt was possible."

We hear this kind of positive report fairly often, but it wasn't always this way. Many people were not raised in a home where prayer was practiced, so they are uncomfortable praying out loud. Add to that the evil intent of our enemy who will do all he can to cause people to feel awkward in prayer, and you have the perfect storm. But you can build your ministry around figuring out how to help people break through and get comfortable with prayer.

Core Belief in People's Desire

It is important to believe that people would love to pray if they were just coached and had someone walk beside them for a while. We schedule events, trainings, schools of prayer, and small groups that are at the basic level for anyone who wants to grow in his or her prayer life.

One of our prayer partners, who couldn't imagine ever praying in public, learned to love prayer ministry through the help of a mentor:

> Well, I haven't been around this prayer ministry that long, and it sure wasn't at the top of my list of things I ever felt God calling me to do. My mentor and I had been talking regularly and he just threw it out as a suggestion, something for me to try out, and at first I thought he was joking. Me? Pray in public? No, I think you have the wrong guy.
>
> But I stepped out in faith, and with my mentor literally holding my hand in the beginning, something inside me soon clicked. All of the stories I'd read in the Bible about God using ordinary, weak people suddenly came alive. It felt like I was one of them almost. I have never looked back.

Ways to Encourage New Pray-ers

We believe prayer ministry is as important as any work in the church, so we challenge the best leaders to join our team. These exceptional people make it work and help us weave these prayer principles throughout our ministry:

Offer easy entry points. We try to have places where people can begin praying that are easy entry points. For example, we hold an annual prayer conference designed to inspire people to get stronger in their prayer lives. We also offer a school of prayer each quarter that is four hours on a Sunday afternoon. We always include introductory topics such as, "How do I pray out loud?" We also add some meatier subjects—for instance, "Learning to pray for wisdom for life."

Gear toward men. I never recruit women to pray. They will come and they will pray! But men will not if the room is all women or if the atmosphere feels too feminine. We go to great lengths to make it male friendly.

Build relationships. I make sure I go to all the men's retreats and the other events, looking for places I can develop men in prayer. Cathy, our associate prayer ministry director, does the same at all the women's events. We connect with people and invite them to the prayer room to experience strategic, measured prayer—and they get hooked. Most of the people on our prayer teams have been recruited by someone and joined out of a trusted relationship.

Make the prayer experience relevant and inspirational. One of the reasons people don't attend prayer events is because they grow tired of praying for sick people. We intentionally don't take prayer requests at many of our events. This approach helps people to realize that the focus in times of corporate prayer is not on them.

One of our major initiatives is helping the other ministries of the church build prayer into their lives, events, and departments. We do our best to be in the planning stages of new campuses or major events so that prayer is part of the DNA of the event—and eventually our church. It takes only a time or two before people begin to see the difference prayer makes in their ministries.

Communicate often and well. We produce a monthly newsletter to more than 2,000 people to inform them about the latest things happening in the prayer world. Most people find out about prayer events through this newsletter—or through Facebook or Twitter.

The truth is that we have a long way to go in the area of prayer. We are not a house of prayer yet in the sense Jesus had in mind. But thankfully we have several wonderful servant ministers who will "not rest until this thing rocks."

PAUL COVERT is pastor of prayer development at prayer pastor at Pure Heart Church and Catalyst Church in Phoenix, AZ, and founder of Threshold Prayer (*thresholdprayer.com*).

12

FACING THE FEAR FACTOR IN CORPORATE PRAYER

- - - - - - - - -

By Kaye Johns

The first time I faced praying out loud in a corporate setting, I was caught in a small group in the back of the room. A young minister instructed everyone to "circle up" for prayer, and I sat there with two other people, face-to-face with my fears. Two people prayed out loud in our group—but I was not one of them!

For more than 20 years now I've been leading prayer groups, but I still understand what it feels like to fear praying aloud. Through trial and error, I've learned some tips that might help you with the groups you lead. You will often encounter fearful people, so here are some suggestions to help them overcome their reluctance.

It's important to help people pray out loud if they've never done it before. If you have a personal story you can tell about yourself when you were first learning to pray out loud, share it! If you talk about your own fears and intimidations, fearful people will see you as an ally.

Then ask them to pick a number from one to five to describe their comfort level in praying out loud (one lowest, five highest). Give them a few seconds to think. Then organize them into groups of two or three to talk about what number on that scale best describes their comfort level in praying aloud. You'll hear friendly chatter and laughter as they learn they are not the only ones who might be uncomfortable or inexperienced.

Give them some rules of thumb to help the prayer time go well. Emphasize the value of one-sentence prayers. I add humor by telling participants that "some people just don't know where to put the period!" I also like to tell people to pray long prayers at home, short prayers in public.

Instruct people to speak up so others can hear them. "If you bow your head," I tell them, "your voice goes into your lap." Then I demonstrate, drawing a few chuckles and making my point.

To alleviate people's worries about what they will pray when it's their turn, I help them understand the importance of praying softly or silently along with the person who is praying. Again, I add a touch of humor by getting people to admit that we all have tried planning our prayers in advance.

Plan ahead and rehearse exactly how you will lead people in prayer. This is very important, both for those who are nervous about praying out loud and for those who will likely take over because they are *too comfortable* praying aloud. Many acronyms work in leading a prayer group into God's presence, but I often choose something simple, such as PTA—Praise, Thanksgiving, Ask.

- *Praise*—Beginning with praise and worship helps people learn to verbalize prayers of worship. Many understand the concept of worshiping with the choir or worship team, but they have not learned to add times of worship to their prayers at home. To prompt their prayers of worship I often use a set of cards with names of Jesus. (Free downloadable masters on our website under products/prayer tips can be printed on cardstock or regular paper: *prayerpowerministries.com*).

- Pass out the prayer cards with Jesus' names, and make sure everyone has one or more. Explain that you will introduce a time of praise and worship first, and they can praise God by His names on their cards. Ask them to complete this sentence, "Father, we praise You as _____." Or "Father, we love You because You are_____."

- *Thanksgiving*—Prayers of thanksgiving are especially easy for people who may be uncomfortable praying aloud. Introduce a time of thanksgiving and ask each of them to thank God for one specific thing by completing the sentence, "Father, I thank You for_____." Most people can come up with a few things—their families, friends, jobs, evidence of God's blessing, His Word, salvation—whatever comes to mind.

- *Ask*—Finally, ask God for what is needed. Let them know what your focus for prayer will be for this session (e.g., the church, the Sunday service, the mission team that's leaving soon, pastoral staff) and go over the topics. Make it clear that you will introduce each topic, and you would like them to pray only about that one topic until you introduce the next one. This again gives parameters, helping those uncomfortable with praying aloud.

Among the many ways to lead corporate prayer, this one will work for those new to the experience. Whatever format you use, stay with it so people will know what to expect. Each time you pray, go over the ground rules and rehearse what you will do. Repetition is important to help people grow comfortable. Don't rush the process, and count on God to bless it.

KAYE JOHNS founded PrayerPower Ministries with her husband Jim in 1994. Their ministry website *prayerpowerministries.com* offers practical prayer materials, many as free downloads.

CHAPTER

13

GO BOLD WITH SMALL GROUP PRAYER

▬ ▬ ▬ ▬ ▬ ▬ ▬ ▬ ▬

By Andrew Wheeler

One of God's stated intents for His Church is that it would be a house of prayer (Isa. 56:7; Matt. 21:13; Mark 11:17; Luke 19:46). As we read through the Book of Acts, we see that the early Church lived up to this expectation. Through prayer, the early believers sought God's wisdom, pled for His intervention, and commissioned His missionaries. God responded to their prayers, guiding their decisions, freeing prisoners, and saving the lost.

Today, we often see a different story. Four "pillars" sustained the early Church: "They devoted themselves to the apostles' teaching and to fellowship, to the breaking of bread and to prayer" (Acts 2:42). In the church today, prayer is often the most neglected pillar.

As a prayer leader, how do you influence the culture of your church to grow in prayer? Service times are closely scheduled. In our busy world, extra prayer meetings struggle to maintain good attendance. Prayer classes attract sparse participation and don't produce lasting change.

How does prayer move beyond a chosen few dedicated individuals to taking root in the entire congregation?

Prayer, Small Groups, and the Church

If your church has a vibrant small group ministry, you have a potential grassroots prayer movement that can change your church's prayer culture. By working together with your small group ministry leaders to promote meaningful, missional prayer throughout your small groups, you can help your church achieve its full potential in prayer.

Most small groups incorporate an element of prayer into their time together. Often, however, that prayer doesn't look beyond the group itself and is relegated to crisis responses rather than focusing on advancing the Kingdom. While personal-crisis prayer is vital in a small group, a steady diet of that is not sufficient to create a balanced, exciting vision for prayer.

You can start creating this vision by working with your small group ministry leaders. Paint a picture of small groups energized with a vision for the church. They already know that lives change in small groups. Help them see how prayer for the church can extend this life change to the congregation as a whole.

Getting Practical

Here are a few ideas to help your small groups incorporate prayer for the church.

- **Church events.** Create a monthly prayer calendar for your church's events. Your church's bulletin probably provides good information to include. Highlight the main events (both weekly and special ones) and suggest a few prayer points for each one.
- **Missionaries.** If your church sends out missionaries, subscribe to their newsletters and compile a regular prayer guide from their prayer letters.
- **Church ministries and leaders.** Contact church staff and key volunteers, asking for prayer requests regarding their ministries. Compile these into a regular prayer guide. Be sure to follow up with them,

passing along answers to prayer. Seeing God answer can encourage small groups to keep praying!

- **Invite a Leader.** Encourage small groups to invite a staff member or key volunteer to visit their group for a time of prayer. Provide a guide for attendees and potential guests, so everyone knows what to expect. In my experience, nothing develops ongoing prayer passion like a time of extended prayer surrounding a church leader.

Spread the Vision

Incorporating prayer for your church into your small groups will benefit your church in many ways. First, you'll grow the prayer lives of your congregation by encouraging prayer that looks beyond the typical personal-crisis prayers to incorporate strategic intercession for your church.

Second, praying for the church will help keep your small groups connected to the church. This connection tends to promote unity in the church and encourage support of your church's leaders and ministries. This can be a great antidote to a spirit of grumbling and discontent within the church.

Third, as God answers prayer, your church's effectiveness will be multiplied. The Book of Exodus records the story of Joshua leading Israel's army against the Amalekites. During this battle, as long as Moses held up his hands in prayer, the Israelite army prevailed. When Moses tired, Aaron and Hur held up his arms, and the army remained victorious (Ex. 17:8–13).

Our prayer team sees our role as that of Aaron and Hur. Church leaders today get weary from serving, just as Moses tired in his service to God. Your church's small groups can lift up their leaders' hands and strengthen them through prayer, inviting God to fight the battles.

ANDREW WHEELER has served as both small group leader and coach in the prayer ministry of Willow Creek Community Church. He is the author of *Together in Prayer* (*togetherinprayer.net*), which is available through *prayershop.org*.

14

HOW TO INSTILL VISION IN YOUR PRAYER GATHERINGS

- - - - - - - - -

By Paul Covert

Have you ever led an agonizingly flat, lifeless prayer meeting? As I've led prayer gatherings during the past 20 years, each gathering had committed and passionate intercessors with the best of intentions, but it became apparent over time that certain pray-ers were getting tired and losing vision.

The intercessor tribe is small; we need to understand this loss of vision. The answer came on a prayer journey in another nation. Our crew met up with a team that starts underground houses of prayer in the Middle East. Not just any prayer squad—the Green Berets of prayer teams. (They are required to pray a couple hours each day!) God is using them to impact the face of the Middle East in prayer.

When their team leader invited us to join their weekly Wednesday night meeting, we were ecstatic. I welcomed the chance to learn how to keep the vision fresh for intercessors over the long haul.

Framing the Vision

Their team leader started the prayer time with a vision statement, something like this: "Tonight we have an incredible opportunity. We get to partner with God for this region of the world. What possibilities are before us! You see, intercession is a very important occupation in the Kingdom of God because it is the job Jesus selected when He ascended into heaven.

Hebrews 7:25 makes that clear: 'He is able to save completely those who come to God through him, *because he always lives to intercede for them*' (emphasis added).

"Jesus could have taken any mission, but He chose intercession. So, it must be important. Tonight, who knows what God will do because we are partnering with Him in prayer!"

The leader closed with another strategic prayer vision statement from Luke 3:21–22: "When all the people were being baptized, Jesus was baptized too. *And as he was praying, heaven was opened* and the Holy Spirit descended on him in bodily form like a dove" (emphasis added). The leader went on to say, "When we enter into prayer like we have tonight, heaven still opens and great works are accomplished."

Vision communicated!

I know this sounds simple. However, framing a powerful vision first has profoundly motivated our intercessors to persist in their prayers over the years.

Scriptural Vision Statements

Armed with this basic principle, I started reading the Bible through, looking for additional prayer vision statements. I found hundreds of them. I marked each verse with the letters *PV* for *prayer vision*.

Here are a few vision statements you might use in your groups:

- In Acts 4:31, *"After they prayed, the place where they were meeting was shaken.* And they were all filled with the Holy Spirit and spoke the word of God boldly" (emphasis added). Tell your group, "Tonight we are gathered to agree in prayer. We are looking for God to shake the walls of heaven and this place through authentic and passionate intercession."

- Revelation 5 describes the Lamb, standing at the center of the throne, encircled by the four living creatures and the elders. When the Lamb takes the scroll from God's hand, the four living creatures and the 24 elders fall down before Him. Verse 8 says, "Each one had a harp and *they were holding golden bowls full of incense, which are the prayers of God's people*" (emphasis added). I believe the living creatures and 24 elders could have held up anything before the Lord. They could have offered the words of a great preacher or the breathtaking beauty of a cathedral, but they chose instead to hold up the prayers of God's people. Urge your intercessors to recognize how this passage magnifies the value of our prayers to God.

- In Acts 16:25–26, Paul and Silas are in jail when they begin to sing and pray: "About midnight Paul and Silas were praying and singing hymns to God, and the other prisoners were listening to them. Suddenly there was such a violent earthquake that *the foundations of the prison were shaken. At once all the prison doors flew open, and everyone's chains came loose*" (emphasis added). Encourage your group with a vision like this: "Tonight we believe that God will topple the barriers and loose us from the chains that are binding us—all by His power."

Using prayer vision statements may not infuse life into every prayer gathering. But I've found that when leaders cast this kind of biblical perspective, our prayer times can change from agonizing to inspiring.

PAUL COVERT is a prayer pastor, regular conference speaker, host of The Threshold Intensive Prayer Conference, and consultant. He has written two books, *Threshold: Transformational Prayer, Transformational Prayer Leadership* and *52 Creative Ways to Pray*, available at *thresholdprayer.com*.

ENGAGING THE FAMILY AND GENERATIONS

15

THINK YOUNG!

- - - - - - - - -

By David Chotka

They were all quite young by our standards. Jesus chose disciples who were just getting started in life. Jesus (who was 30–31 at the time) picked 12- to 24-year-olds and trained them for two of His three-year ministry. Then, 11 of those 12 disciples went on to transform the inhabited world with His teaching—empowered by His Spirit and employing the same method of discipleship.

The root of everything that Jesus did was His prayer life. Jesus deliberately prayed before He acted. In fact, John's gospel tells us that He could do nothing unless the Father showed Him (John 5:19, 30). After a night of prayer, the Father revealed His leader core—and they were young (Luke 6:12-13).

The 12 young disciples were so intrigued by the prayer life of Jesus that they asked Him to teach them how He did it (Luke 11:1). They had seen prayer before, but never prayer that had the effect that Jesus' praying did. He raised the dead, healed the sick, taught unearthly truth, and was transfigured before their eyes.

Earth-Changing Strategy

Jesus' discipling strategy was simple. What did He do? He picked teenagers and young adults—and taught them to pray (and obey) like Him.

This was a vital, dynamic prayer of encounter. This was prayer that clearly heard the voice of God, discerned the action of God and then entered into it, accomplishing wonders to the astonishment of all. In fact, Jesus refused to act unless He had a clear, direct leading, a command from God for every action.

He did not merely speak to God, but He heard God interacting with Him back and forth until the fellowship (and/or the assignment) was complete. Jesus taught the Twelve to do this.

He mentored young Peter to hear the voice of God—and obey. (The conversations between Jesus and Peter are some of the most instructive and warmly human accounts we have from the Gospels.) He also brought three young adults with Him to learn together.

Peter, James, and John were there when He prayed to raise a little girl from the dead. When Jesus prayed about His future, talked with Moses and Elijah, and was transfigured, they were witnesses. And they were there when He was prayed in death-anguish in Gethsemane. Even in grief, He was teaching them to pray like He did.

And He worked with nine more "20-somethings" in the same way. Then there were 58 others in the group called "the 70," who also followed him. Jesus required them to watch and learn and do as He did. Then He sent them out two by two to practice what they had learned.

Most of Jesus' time was given over to instructing teenagers and young adults. God sent His Son to spend enormous amounts of His time with them during His ministry. By doing this, He gave them (and us) a method that could be easily replicated.

Here it is:

- Develop your prayer life to hear God (without this step none of the others apply).
- Ask the Lord to lead you to teenagers and young adults to learn to hear the Lord with you.

- Mentor one, three, and 12 at a time in how you hear and obey the Lord.
- Hear and obey God in front of them.
- Send them out to do the same and report the results back to you.
- Celebrate the successes, correct the failures. Laugh together.
- Instruct them to find one, three, and 12 others to disciple.
- Then start over again yourself with a new group.

Think Younger

As a prayer leader, are you struggling to get people to join together in prayer? Maybe you need to think younger. Ask the Lord to show you some teens or college-aged adults in your church and pour yourself into training them to pray effectively.

That was Jesus' method. We would be wise to imitate it.

DAVID CHOTKA is lead pastor of Spruce Grove Alliance Church in Alberta, Canada, the head of prayer ministry in his denomination, and the author of *Power Praying*.

MAKING THE NEXT GENERATION A PRIORITY

By Camden McAfee

Y ou've probably heard that 59 percent of young Christians temporarily or permanently disconnect from the church after age 15. You've probably heard that suicide is the third leading cause of death for youth ages 10–24. You've probably heard that a quarter of teenagers have at least one major episode of depression in high school.

These numbers aren't just statistics; they're my peers. As part of this next generation, I need to ask, are you praying for this generation, knowing we're the ones to inherit the Church in the coming decades?

Unprecedented Opportunity

What an opportunity we have before us! Young people aren't a burden to be borne; they're a generation to be activated. Consider the ways God has used young people in the past to shape the direction of nations.

At the age of 26, George Whitefield expanded the impact of the First

Great Awakening in America. Before Charles Spurgeon was 20, he had preached more than 600 sermons. Evan Roberts, the central figure of the Welsh Revival, was only 26 when God used him to carry the message of revival to an entire nation.

God is passionate about using young people to further His Kingdom on earth. As the Church, we need to learn how to pray for the next generation and how to mobilize prayer for them. The need and the opportunity are set before us; it's time for us to pray.

Praying for More

God wants so much for my generation. Nick Hall, in his book *Reset: Jesus Changes Everything* (*pulsemovement.com*), suggests eight areas in which the next generation needs prayer. I've adapted them here:

- **Faith.** For those who have walked away from Jesus, pray for their faith to be restored and strengthened. For those who are following Him, pray for their faith to grow even more.
- **Plans.** The decisions young people make will affect them for the rest of their lives. Pray for God to direct their plans away from evil and toward good.
- **Self-Image.** Many young people struggle with feelings of worthlessness. Pray for the love of God to surround and fill those struggling with self-image.
- **Relationships.** Broken relationships plague this generation. Pray for restoration of relationships with family, friends, and God.
- **Purity.** Pray for a restoration and renewed vision of purity for this generation. Pray for any shame to be removed by the love of Jesus.
- **Habits.** Destructive habits further drive my generation from God. Pray not only for the removal of old habits but for the establishment of new, God-honoring practices.
- **Affections.** At the root of our habits are affections. Pray for God to awaken a deep longing only He can fill in this generation—and pray for Him to satisfy our affections in Jesus.

- **Generation.** Finally, pray this generation will experience awakening and revival from coast to coast. Jesus longs for my generation not only to know Him but to spread His gospel around the world.

Mobilizing Next-Generation Prayer

Knowing the *need* to pray for the next generation and *how* to pray for us, what are some ways to incorporate this into what you're already doing as prayer leaders? Here are a few simple suggestions:

1. Pray for the next generation regularly. Incorporate prayer for the next generation into your prayer group. Maybe this means a little each time, or maybe it means taking one night to focus solely on the next generation. I encourage you to pray monthly for the needs of young people.
2. Create intergenerational relationships in your church. Meet and get to know a young person or couple at your church. Learn about them. Invite them to lunch. Ask how you can pray for them. Begin to build these "prayer bridges" in relationship between generations.
3. Partner in prayer. Invite young people to join you in prayer. Consider ways you can adapt your group to accommodate their needs. Commit yourself to sharing the baton of prayer with the next generation.

The choice before us is clear. We can either ignore the cries of a generation, or we can do the hard work of praying for them and engaging with them. The brokenness the enemy means for evil can be turned around and used by God for good.

CAMDEN McAFEE is writer for Pulse, an evangelistic organization that exists to awaken culture to the reality of Jesus (*pulsemovement.com*), especially among the next generation.

17

CREATIVE INTERGENERATIONAL PRAYER GATHERINGS

— — — — — — — —

By Kim Butts

In our increasingly dark and seductive culture, how well are we discipling children and youth in prayer? Are we teaching them to seek Jesus and listen to *His* voice instead of other potentially dangerous voices around them? As adults, we need to impart what we have learned about the purpose and power of prayer.

In visits to hundreds of churches over the past two decades, I have seen very few congregations that intentionally include children or entire families in their corporate prayer gatherings. Rarely have I seen youth from middle school or high school involved.

However, when churches initiate creative prayer experiences, families and people of all ages can become fully engaged, meeting with God in new, fresh ways. Instead of viewing prayer as a perfunctory act or a duty, they discover it to be a delight. This is especially true when the prayer experience crosses generations.

I believe the lack of intergenerational prayer is robbing the Lord's Church of her power and Kingdom purpose. Remember that children do not have a junior Holy Spirit. Youth and children are fully capable of engaging in the deep things of God! Do not marginalize them spiritually—especially in prayer.

Creative Prayer Experiences

Prayer leaders and pastors can employ simple strategies to help their churches become intergenerational praying churches. Here are some ideas:

- **Prayer Stations:** Develop prayer stations to engage everyone in creative prayer. Allow for people to move from one station to the next in their own time. For more detailed information, look up "prayer stations" on Pinterest, or email *kim@harvestprayer.com*.

- **Kingdom Praying:** Praying through the Scriptures helps people to see the difference between our "default" mode of prayer—which is largely focused on oneself or the health needs of others—and praying the purposes of God. As we incorporate Scripture, we see that God is interested in things like Christian unity (John 17:11), love for one another (John 13:34–35), and sending workers into the harvest field (Matt. 9:37–38).

- **Prayer Encounters/Prayer Parties:** This is a fun way to engage families and teach prayer concepts at the same time. Offer several short prayer activities that a family can do together around a table. For instance, provide a map or globe and let each family member choose a country. Pray for all of the children and teens who are orphans, who live in poverty, or who live in families torn apart by war. Making a paper chain (using one link for each nation), and then taking the chain home, can serve as a reminder to continue praying.

- **Bless a Pastor:** Using sticky notes, write some prayers including specific ways you want God to bless your pastor or a church leader. When finished, the whole family can get up and "stick it to the pastor" or whomever they have chosen to bless in prayer.

- **Body Prayer:** Together look up Scriptures that describe how several people in the Bible prayed from various body postures. Bowing our heads and folding our hands are not the only ways to seek God with our bodies. Postures help to describe the attitudes of our hearts at various times. (See Abraham in Gen. 17:3, 17; Moses in Ex. 9:27–29; King Solomon in 1 Kings 8:54, and Jesus in Mark 6:41 and John 11:41, 17:1). Talk about how emotions can affect the ways we choose to use our bodies in prayer. What posture expresses humility? Which is a posture of expectation? How can we use our bodies to pray with thankfulness?

- **Prayer and the Senses:** Create ways to pray that use each of the senses. Write the names of people in sand as you pray for them. Or pray as you listen to worship music. Give thanks to God as you "taste and see" that He is good (different kinds of finger foods). Smell flowers or spices and give God praise for all He has created.

- **Praying in Color:** Draw your prayers to the Lord with markers or crayons. This is especially good for young children who can't read or write yet.

- **Praying the World:** Ahead of time, create passports that each child or family can use as they move around the room, praying for missionaries and the nations/people groups they serve. Stamp the passports at each station.

The creativity of our God allows us so much freedom of expression in prayer! He wants all of His people to seek His face. With a bit of creativity, you can connect all the generations with the heart of the Father—and significantly grow the prayer movement in your church.

KIM BUTTS, a contributing writer to *Prayer Connect*, is the co-founder of Harvest Prayer Ministries (*harvestprayer.com*).

THE POWER OF FAMILY PRAYER

By Cheryl Sacks

A number of years ago I had a powerful vision of our nation shrouded in darkness. Suddenly, a single home started to glow with living light, which then spread to others, rapidly transforming the entire country! Then I heard the voice of the Lord say, *Revival will come to America when the family altar is restored.*

I believe with all my heart that we are now in the awakening moment I saw in my vision: God is about to visit the families of America.

When God spoke those words to me, I was standing on the platform in my home church, having just finished speaking in a conference on "Revival and the Holy Spirit." Not one of the speakers had mentioned family prayer. And I wasn't sure if something as simple as families praying together could transform a nation. So I asked the Lord to confirm if He was really speaking to me.

At that moment, a young man walked to the microphone and began to pray, echoing the words I had just heard: "Lord, restore the family altar in homes across America."

Timeless Principles

This encounter with the Lord took me on a journey to learn more about the power of family prayer. One day I ran across a book titled *How to Have a Family Altar.* Even though the book was written in the early 1950s, its principles are timeless. One story confirmed further what God had been speaking to me:

> The 17th century Scottish church leader, Thomas Boston, was burdened over the cold spiritual state of his church. It was not only cold, but practically empty. He decided that the way to bring revival to his church and community was to establish family prayer in every home. He went from home to home, leading people to Christ and encouraging families to pray daily together. After nearly three years, revival fires were burning in his church, and large numbers of joy-filled believers and seekers of God crowded into the church every Sunday![1]

In today's world of busy schedules and digital distractions, it's hard for families to find time to eat dinner together, let alone pray together. Yet praying together deepens relationships, alleviates arguing and fighting, and strengthens family ties more than any single thing we can do.

Launching Family Prayer

Many believe that creating a new, lasting habit takes at least a month. That's why I encourage church leaders to launch a month-long campaign to help families jumpstart a lifetime of praying together.

Here are some ideas from my own experience, along with great advice from pastors and prayer leaders:

- Frank Nevarez, pastor of Emmanuel Fellowship, Cottonwood, AZ, says, "Launch your family prayer campaign and give it a unique name and theme." He dedicated an entire month to teaching on family prayer and encouraging families to pray together daily.
- Select a resource for your church family to read together, such as

Kim Butts's book, *The Praying Family*, or my new book, *The Prayer-Saturated Family: How to Change the Atmosphere in Your Home Through Prayer.* These are full of ideas to engage the whole family in prayer.

- Kevin Hartke, pastor of Trinity Christian Fellowship, Chandler, AZ, successfully engaged Sunday school classes in a family prayer campaign. Everyone read through a book on family prayer and then discussed how they could put its principles into action in their own homes.
- During a family prayer campaign, give your families an assignment, such as praying through the 31-Day Family Prayer Guide found in *The Prayer-Saturated Family.* This book has creative ideas and scriptural prayer models to jumpstart or strengthen family prayer.
- Initiate a citywide campaign. Prayer leader Jason Hubbard in Bellingham, WA, bought books on family prayer for the 60 pastors and church prayer coordinators in his network and launched a month of family prayer across their entire city.
- Seek support on the state level. In Phoenix, in response to our request, Arizona Governor Doug Ducey issued a proclamation designating January National Family Prayer Month.

Giving time and effort to your church families' growth in the Lord and the spiritual climate of their homes is one of the best investments you can make! Healthy families create healthy churches, healthy schools, and healthy communities.

[1]Norman V. Williams, *How to Have a Family Prayer Altar* (Chicago, IL: Moody Press, 1951), 9.

CHERYL SACKS is a national speaker and the co-founder and leader of BridgeBuilders International Leadership Network (*bridgebuilders.net*). She is the author of three books that are available at *prayershop.org*.

19

"BUT LORD, I'VE NEVER TAUGHT CHILDREN BEFORE!"

By Cynthia Hyle Bezek

Probably the most common frustration I hear from church prayer leaders goes like this: "Someone [fill in the blank: my pastor, home group leader, Sunday school teacher, the elders, the deacons, the women's ministry director] ought to be mobilizing prayer, but they aren't! How can I encourage them to get on board?"

There is no simple answer to this common complaint. If someone in leadership doesn't have a vision, passion, or confidence for prayer, all the hints, invitations, requests, nagging, or even bribing in the world won't change them. Your best resort is to pray for them and humbly set a good example.

I knew all that. Still, I found myself thinking along those lines last fall. The church prayer ministry I help lead invited our children to pray for our pastors one Sunday during Clergy Appreciation Month. The kids went forward, circled around the pastors—and were utterly silent. Were they just shy? Or did they actually not know how to pray? We were concerned. And, I confess, my first thought was to wonder how we could get our children's ministry on board in prayer.

That's when the Holy Spirit reminded some of us in our prayer ministry that He had called *us* to lead the way in prayer for our church.

But Lord! I have never taught children before! I am not gifted with children! In fact, I'm sort of afraid of them—at least groups of them! Send someone else.

It's Up to Us

You probably can guess how that went. God wasn't planning to send someone else. He wanted us to do it. As it so happened, I had already written a children's prayer curriculum (oddly enough, I can write for children—I'm just inexperienced teaching them!) and our prayer ministry had several people who are gifted teachers. So we volunteered to teach eight weeks on prayer during the children's church hour. The children's ministry director was delighted to have prayer taught—and to give her volunteers a break. We had her full and enthusiastic support.

Our curriculum included lessons on basics (prayer equals relationship with God, the Lord's Prayer, and intercession) as well as more advanced concepts like listening prayer, perseverance, and inner-healing prayer. One of our prayer ministry members (an experienced teacher) took the lead in planning the lesson each week. Men and women on our team took turns telling the story. And the remainder of the prayer ministry members supported them by interceding for the children and leading small groups of two or three children each week.

My first week as a small-group leader I was nervous. To my relief, however, I found the children to be engaged and responsive. They opened their hearts to the Lord and to us—and they seemed to catch on faster than adults often do. So, after my first-week jitters, I actually looked forward to being with the kids.

Actually, I was amazed at some of their responses. Some tough-looking little boys shared some pretty big hurts. A child with learning difficulties volunteered to write his prayer on the poster board up front. After a lesson on listening prayer from John 10, every single child heard something encouraging from the Good Shepherd.

In the unit on persevering prayer, a little girl (we'll call her Tanya) told me she had been praying for a long time about a friend who is mean to her. Tanya said that at first all she asked God to do was to "make her nicer." But as Tanya persisted in prayer, she started to realize some things. She realized the other little girl might be nicer if she knew Jesus! So, Tanya started praying that her friend would come to know Jesus. But then Tanya realized that her friend might not even have heard very much about Jesus, so Tanya started praying that the other girl would read the Bible so she could get to know Jesus.

Over time, as she persevered in prayer and let God reshape her prayers, her prayers became more mature and others-focused. She told me her prayers are not so "greedy" anymore. I realized that this little girl understood more about listening to God, persevering in prayer, and Kingdom-praying than many adults I know!

I'm so glad our prayer ministry didn't wait for somebody else to come along and teach our kids to pray. God gave *us* the ministry of prayer for our church. Why shouldn't we be the ones He uses to help the kids learn to talk to Him?

CYNTHIA HYLE BEZEK served as managing editor and editor of *Pray!* magazine from 2002 until it ceased publication in 2009. She is author of *Prayer Begins with Relationship* and *Come Away with Me: Pray! Magazine's Guide to Prayer Retreats,* both published by NavPress.

WHERE ARE THE PRAYING MEN?

By Mark Price

They came every Thursday night. They prayed facedown, stretched out before the altar, sometimes for an hour or two. This small group of men called out to God for personal and corporate needs.

This was my first pastorate, and I was convinced of the importance of praying men. Of course, having women engaged in prayer is just as important. In fact, they are often the faithful intercessors in any church. But I was particularly burdened to mobilize the men.

So, each week, five or six men gathered and prayed. I was not discouraged at the attendance because I remembered the story of Jeremiah Lanphier. In 1857, in response to his invitation to the first official New York City noonday prayer meeting, only six businessmen showed up. However, those few eventually grew into groups of tens of thousands meeting daily to pray. In that first pastorate, my prayer was, "Do it again, Lord. Do it again!"

Our Thursday night prayer meeting continued for two years with the same five or six men showing up and crying out to God. After a ministry move to another church, I continued to press the need for praying men. I asked them to join me on Thursday nights to pray—and this time just two came. Again, the story of Lanphier and the revival of 1857 helped deflect my potential discouragement. We changed our prayer time to Sunday mornings before our service. Our participants then ranged from two to six men.

But throughout this time, I kept wondering, *Where are the praying men?* I have preached and taught numerous Bible studies on prayer. So where are the men who have caught the vision, passion, and burden for prayer?

E.M. Bounds, in his classic work, *Prayer and Praying Men*, writes, "Old Testament history is filled with accounts of praying saints. The leaders of Israel in those early days were noted for their praying habits. Prayer is the one thing which stands out prominently in their lives."[1]

Change in Perspective

The more I wondered, the more I fought discouragement. As I expressed this to the Lord, He showed me things I had forgotten. He reminded me to stay focused on what *was* happening in the church, instead of just looking at what I thought *wasn't* happening to my satisfaction.

So, I began to take inventory of the prayer life of our church. The Lord reminded me of the small group of women who meet frequently on Saturday mornings to pray. The four men who pray on Wednesday mornings. The women who gather at the church to pray for the public schools in our city—and those who partner with each other to pray for marriages. Then there are the women's prayer team, the deacons, and the staff who are available for personal prayer after the service.

In my discouragement I had also discounted the importance of our church prayer coordinator who sends emails daily with a devotional thought that encourages members to pray. She also organizes prayer events such as the National Day of Prayer. The church maintains a prayer group database that sends prayer requests to the membership as requests come into the church office.

And to top it off—the church has invested money to establish a prayer room readily accessible from the worship center.

Change in Heart

I realized that although I have not seen large numbers of men committed to prayer, an atmosphere of prayer is present in our church. We've even heard people from outside our church comment, "I hear you are a praying church. I have a request."

So instead of focusing on my seemingly failed expectations, I will commit to leading my church toward developing an even greater atmosphere of prayer in these ways:

- As pastor, I will continue to model and teach the importance and activity of prayer.
- We will always have a prayer coordinator to demonstrate that prayer is our priority.
- We will provide numerous opportunities to engage people in prayer.
- We will take time to give reports of answered prayer.

Yes, I will always remember that group of men praying facedown, stretched out before the altar. And certainly, I want more men to join me in prayer today as well. But I am thankful for a church with a few men and a few women who are obedient to Jesus' desire for His Church to be a house of prayer.

God responds when His people pray—and it isn't about the numbers.

[1]E.M. Bounds, *Prayer and Praying Men* in *The Complete Works of E.M. Bounds on Prayer* (Grand Rapids: Baker Book House, 1990), 497.

MARK PRICE is pastor of Southside Baptist Church in Tyler, TX, and adjunct instructor in the Certificate in Ministry program at East Texas Baptist University.

CREATING SPECIAL PRAYER EMPHASES

MAKING SENSE OF ALL THOSE DAYS OF PRAYER

By Jonathan Graf

What's a prayer leader to do? There seem to be too many days of prayer: National Day of Prayer, Global Day of Prayer, International Day of Prayer for the Persecuted Church, Day of Prayer for the Peace of Jerusalem, and Day of Prayer for Children at Risk. And those are just *some* of the events clamoring for our participation.

Then there are the initiatives—Seek God for the City, Praying through the 10/40 Window, 30 Days of Prayer for the Muslim World, 30 Days of Prayer for the Hindu World, and PrayWorld.

And what about the ongoing calls to prayer—First Friday, the Presidential Prayer Team, Hollywood Prayer Network—to say nothing of denominational prayer emphases your church should highlight?

A church can only focus on so much. As a prayer leader, how can you make choices about what you should participate in—and what you can forego?

Seek God and Discern

Each church will be different in its needs, so my broad answer is that you need to genuinely seek God for His desires for your church. But let me suggest some guidelines that may help you discern which events your church should participate in.

1. Use the National Prayer Accord principles. The National Prayer Accord was originally devised by Jonathan Edwards and others prior to the First Great Awakening. Their intention was that each church would pray around the same basic theme of revival. But churches would also pray weekly or monthly in their own circles, quarterly with other churches in their community, and nationally once a year. A prayer rhythm focused this way is a pattern easily handled.

Make participation in the National Day of Prayer and/or the Global Day of Prayer as your once-a-year emphasis. Then look for three other times you can join with other churches in your community for a prayer event. Select a concert of prayer to highlight praying for your community. Or choose some of the other days to participate together.

2. Select by tiers of importance. What seems to be a fit for the personality of your church? Is your church a strong missions church? Then you will want to use at least one missions focus. Does your church seem to have a strong heart for Israel? Then certainly highlight the Day of Prayer for the Peace of Jerusalem.

3. Select by levels of effort. Another way to proceed is to choose at least one or two initiatives that take some effort to organize—and then add anything else that can be done with ease. For example, select a prayer initiative like Seek God for the City or one of many 40 Days of Prayer. These will take some promotional effort, but the rewards of participation are enormous for your church. A prayer initiative for your congregation will bring long-term results of more interest in prayer.

As a prayer leader, however, you can only handle one or maybe two prayer events per year that require this level of effort. But you can highlight other events throughout the year that do not take effort. For example, even if you can't spearhead a National Day of Prayer event, you can certainly publicize other prayer gatherings in your community on that day. While you might not be able to do a big event around the Day of Prayer for Children at Risk, you can get information and prayer guides to people who might be interested in participating. And praying for Hollywood might not involve your entire church, but you can provide guides for those who have a burden for the entertainment industry.

4. What does your leadership want? Another possible plan of attack is to gather your pastor(s) and key leaders each fall and review all the possible prayer events you can participate in during the coming year. Before such a meeting, gather all the information you can on every possible day and be ready to make your recommendations. Talk as a group about each one, and together map out the year.

One possible starting point for gathering information is past issues of *Prayer Connect* magazine (or the website *prayerconnect.net*). Many of the possible prayer events in a calendar year are listed.

While there are a lot of possibilities, don't be overwhelmed! Seek the Lord and plan ahead. Then watch what happens as you take advantage of these calls to prayer.

JONATHAN GRAF is publisher of *Prayer Connect* and president of The Church Prayer Leaders Network (*prayerleader.com*).

HOW TO GROW A VISION FOR REVIVAL

- - - - - - - -

By Bob Bakke

M y friend, Byron Paulus of Life Action Ministries, describes revival this way: "When God comes in revival, He accomplishes in a brief time what would normally take many years. Revival is the intensifying, accelerating, multiplying, and magnifying work of God."

I like this. Given the social, political, and ethical chaos today, combined with the weakness of the Church, many believers are hungry for such an intense season of unrestrained grace against which the human heart and society is defenseless.

Confidence in the efficacy of revival assumes a confidence in God to accomplish what He wills—in the power of His Spirit, for the glory of His Son, in answer to the prayers of His people. But the hope of revival also assumes that God is *willing* to send revival in answer to our cries.

Revival Hindrances

How do we grow this vision within the local church? First, we acknowledge that we're prone to believe these myths:

- that our problems are unique
- that the Church and the world have never faced problems like ours
- that God is either disinterested or too disgusted to help.

We also forget that such weary seasons in the Church and troubled times in culture have appeared time and time again since Adam. When we face the need for revival, our forgetfulness can lead to panic, hysterics, paralysis, or despair—as if our problems have left us alone and adrift in unknown waters without a compass.

We need to repent of this forgetfulness. It is a product of pride. When it comes to growing a vision for revival, the remedies don't change, even though our historical context evolves. The remedies are essentially consistent and quite simple. They aren't *easy*, just simple.

Revival Forerunners

A case in point is Arnold Dallimore's remarkable biography of George White-field and the history of The Great Awakening in the 1730s and '40s. Whitefield was characterized by his contemporaries as a comet across the sky of history. Countless people were transformed in his wake. But God began laying the foundations for this so-called "Great Awakening" some 60 years before.

Dallimore records the story of Dr. Anthony Horneck of London who was a leader in the Church of England. In 1673, Horneck was alarmed at the listless and sinful church in London. So, he "preached a number of what he called 'awakening sermons.' As a result, several young men began to meet together weekly in order to build up one another in the Christian faith. They gathered in small groups at certain fixed locations and their places of meeting became known as Society rooms. In these gatherings they read the Bible . . . and prayed; they also went out among the poor to relieve want at their own expense and to show kindness to all. . . . The work grew so that by 1730 nearly one hundred of these [Prayer] Societies existed in London, and others—perhaps another hundred—were to be found in cities and towns throughout England. The Societies movement became, in many senses, the cradle of the Revival."[1]

Does the pattern ring a bell?

- Someone with the conviction and power of God's Spirit urgently reminds the people of God about the primacy of God, His Word, and His Savior, Jesus Christ.
- Small groups respond with united and ongoing prayer and intentionally disperse into the streets of the city.
- The Lord adds to the number of those who are saved.
- Ultimately, history is transformed.

Simple Remedies

We know from the Bible and Church history the fundamental ingredients to grow a vision for revival in your congregation:

- Pray for a spirit of prayer to fall upon your church. Pray especially that your senior pastor will be known as the leader of such praying.
- Remind people of the Bible stories of the Spirit's transforming work in the history of Israel and the Church. You can find these stories on sites such as *onecry.com*.
- Tell current stories of ways the Spirit is reviving and awakening today. You can find these accounts at *cbn.com*, for example.
- Start small groups for prayer, praying specifically for revival.

Remember, it may take 60 years before the flood comes. But be encouraged and confident in two things: God will answer, and you are the first part of His answer.

[1]George Whitefield. *The Life and Times of the Great Evangelist of the Eighteenth-Century Revival.* Vol. 2. (Westchester, IL: Cornerstone Books, 1979), 29.

BOB BAKKE is senior teaching pastor of Hillside Church of Bloomington, MN. He is also on the executive leadership team of OneCry and a member of America's National Prayer Committee.

23

INTEGRATING WORSHIP WITH PRAYER

- - - - - - - - -

By Daniel Henderson

All my life, worship services have seemed basically the same. Of course, some stylistic elements have changed. Hymnbooks have been replaced with modern song lyrics projected on a screen. Keyboards and guitars have taken center stage. ProPresenter software images and video clips frequently appear. Pews have disappeared in favor of theater seating. Large wood pulpits have given way to smaller stands—or nothing at all.

In spite of these changes, few elements have changed in the vast majority of worship services. The essential components usually occur in the same order: singing, then preaching, interspersed with occasional prayer and announcements. The service divides neatly into two segments—worship in music and worship in the Word. Prayer is typically a seasoning lightly sprinkled on the gathering.

Why So Segmented?

Who says it has to be this way? Here is a radical proposal that might change how we worship on Sundays. Instead of 20 minutes of music followed by 40 minutes of preaching, zipped up neatly with an opening and closing prayer, imagine the service looking more like this:

- Worship in song—8 minutes
- First preaching segment—12 minutes
- Praying together about what we have just heard—5 minutes
- Short worship song—3 minutes
- Second teaching segment—15 minutes
- Praying together about what we have just heard—5 minutes
- Short worship song—3 minutes
- Third teaching segment—10 minutes
- Praying together about what we have just heard—5 minutes
- Worship and response—7 minutes
- Worship through giving and ministry announcements—5 minutes
- Final worship—3 minutes.

Some may immediately object, arguing that shorter teaching segments compromise the Word in some way. Of course, Scripture is clear that we must accurately teach and passionately preach God's inspired Word. However, if you time how long it takes to read some of the New Testament sermons, you will find they are shorter and more effective than most sermons in our churches today. (See Acts 2:4–41, 4:8–12; 7:2–53.)

Benefits of Integration

I see several benefits to an approach such as the one I suggested:

1. Attention. Like it or not, the attention span of Americans is getting shorter. Research shows that with all the technological multitasking we practice via smartphones, iPads, and email, our brains are actually being remapped, making activities that require extended focus more difficult.

Shorter components in our church services, punctuated with prayerful application and worship, might encourage better focus and engagement. I remember attending a church where the sermons typically lasted 55–65 minutes. I suspect that after 50 minutes few people could even remember what was said at the beginning of the sermon.

2. Interaction. We have become a spectator culture when it comes to worship. Even when we sing, we give our attention to the performers on the platform. We passively listen to extended messages with very little crowd participation.

Taking time to pray and worship in connection with shorter segments of teaching and response helps our minds and hearts engage via the power of God's Word. Contextually appropriate expressions of prayer give worshipers the opportunity to connect with one another at a meaningful level. This could include private prayer, small group prayer, prayer led from the front, and other formats.

3. Application. Recently, I heard a senior pastor say, "I've become convinced that the most powerful way to apply God's Word is to pray it." I agree. Within a worshiping community even the opportunity to sing songs related to the theme of a teaching segment can inspire us to engage with the truth.

- The goal of teaching is to engage the mind and heart in order to affect the will, which, in turn, leads to deeper application and obedience.
- The goal of singing is to use our whole being to extol the character of God with a keen awareness of His presence.
- Substantive prayer, woven into the service, enhances all of these goals.

A more interactive experience will likely threaten some who are satisfied with the status quo. However, the boldness to try a different, more engaging approach might produce a different result. And a different result might shape a different kind of disciple, leading to different kind of impact on the world that so desperately needs to encounter passionate, pure, and powerful believers walking in the light of Jesus Christ.

DANIEL HENDERSON is the president and founder of Strategic Renewal, a ministry that exists to ignite personal renewal, congregational revival, and leadership restoration (*strategicrenewal.com*).

24

TIPS TO CREATE A SCRIPTURE-BASED PRAYER GUIDE

-- -- -- -- --

By Sandra Higley

P raying God's Word is powerful. Like-minded believers approaching God's throne of grace in unified, Spirit-led prayer make twice the impact. But how can we get everyone praying together in one accord?

One way is to create a Scripture-based prayer guide that gives people a reference point to direct or redirect their thoughts as everyone seeks God's face together.

As you prepare your guide, you need some essential tools. In addition to your Bible, you'll want a concordance, topical index, or online Bible program with a search engine. Resources include: *biblegateway.com*, *biblehub.com*, and *biblestudytools.com*. You can also type the subject directly into your search engine to find examples in Scripture.

Guide Preparation

Here are some tips to consider as you let the Holy Spirit lead you in preparing such a guide:

1. Get rid of your agenda and replace it with God's. We may believe we've been led by the Spirit to pray in a particular way, but those prayers must align with God's heart. George Müller said, "The Spirit and the Word must be combined. If I look to the Spirit alone without the Word, I lay myself open to great delusions also. If the Holy Ghost guides us at all, He will do it according to the Scriptures and never contrary to them."[1]

2. Broaden your perspective and find common ground. Rather than create a prayer guide asking God to have the building committee vote to expand the fellowship hall, for instance, acknowledge that God's plan may lead in an entirely different direction. Find Scriptures that acknowledge His will, ask for wisdom, and bless the people entrusted with the decision to hear His voice—no matter what.

3. Find Scripture that directs you to pray through tough things. Giving thanks can be hard when your group is facing dire circumstances. But thankfulness provides a firm foundation for the requests yet to come. Let the scriptural instruction flow into the next Scripture and the next to create your prayer.

Example: "Father, You have told us that it is Your will that we give thanks in every circumstance (1 Thess. 5:18). That's really hard to do. But we choose to thank You because You are good and Your love toward us endures forever" (1 Chron. 16:34).

4. Find a similar scenario in the Bible. Let the dynamics of that situation direct you to verses that will lead you through your situation. What was the person experiencing or feeling during that time? Can you sense the greatest needs in that circumstance?

Example: Perhaps you are praying for someone who is suffering. You might pick Scriptures regarding Job's or Paul's experiences that will lead you through prayers for perseverance, assurance of God's love, faithful friends, Kingdom warfare, or God's glory.

5. Keep coming back to God's character. Use Scripture that acknowledges God's attributes.

Example: "Father, we acknowledge that You are Alpha and Omega—You know the beginning and You know the end (Rev. 22:13). This truth and the fact that You are love (1 John 4:8) assures us that Your plans for this situation are good (Ps. 145:9).

6. Sift through the prayer request to affirm what you know to be true in Scripture. Rather than praying that X-Y-Z would stop, repeat back to God what you know to be true.

Example: "Father, we know that You are actively orchestrating all the details of our lives for our good (Rom. 8:28). The enemy may be trying to take us down with what's happening right now, but we know that You are achieving far more than we can imagine (Eph. 3:20–21). We humbly ask that You remove this difficulty from us, but if that is not Your will, we rejoice in Your never-ending grace" (2 Cor. 12:8–9).

7. Find "so that" Scriptures to turn into prayers. The apostle Paul frequently prayed for one thing so that another would occur. An example of one of Paul's "so that" prayers is Philippians 1:9–11. To focus your prayers, use Scripture that shares a process and a result.

Example: "Father, we know that Your Word will always accomplish what You purpose (Isa. 55:11). Help us to stay in Your Word so that transformation will occur" (Rom. 12:2).

Writing a Scripture-based prayer guide will become easier the more you do it. Keep a notebook handy as you spend time in God's Word and jot down Scriptures that can easily be turned into a prayer for future use. Above all, ask God to direct your thoughts and bring them into alignment with His will.

[1]George Mueller, *Answers to Prayer* (Chicago: Moody, 2007), 14.

SANDRA HIGLEY was one of the founders of *Pray!* magazine. While at NavPress she wrote many popular Scripture-based prayer guides, including *Targeted Prayers for Your Church*, available from *prayershop.org*.

25

MOTIVATING AND MOBILIZING EVANGELISTIC PRAYER

- - - - - - - - -

By Elaine Helms

W hile working as a church prayer coordinator and as a national prayer leader, I learned that Christians do not automatically pray for the lost. Many are lulled into complacency, believing that everyone lives in a safety zone until they choose to follow either Jesus or the devil. Scripture, however, does not validate that. Rather, because of Adam's sin, we are all born in captivity to the devil.

Therefore, we need to give believers a biblical foundation about the condition of those without Christ. We must address the *why* before the *how to*.

Condition of the Lost

Jesus says in John 12:46, "I have come into the world as a light, so that no one who believes in me should stay in darkness." Paul says in Romans 5:8 and 18: "But God demonstrates his own love for us in this: While we were still sinners, Christ died for us. Consequently, just as one trespass resulted in condemnation for all people, so also one righteous act resulted in justification and life for all people."

Condition of the Christian's Heart

In Romans 9:1–3, Paul says, "I speak the truth in Christ—I am not lying, my conscience confirms it through the Holy Spirit—I have great sorrow and unceasing anguish in my heart. For I could wish that I myself were cursed and cut off from Christ for the sake of my people, those of my own race."

With this verse in mind, we have to ask, "Do we feel that kind of grief? Do we care enough to pray for the lost? When was the last time we lost sleep, staying up all night weeping before the Lord, asking God to draw our family members, neighbors, and/or friends to Jesus?"

Discovering Lost People

Before we can pray for the lost, we must discover lost people around us. One method for raising awareness is to hand out index cards.

Ask members of your prayer group to write numbers on the card. Then, make a list: #1, the name of their neighbor to the right; #2, the name of their neighbor on the left; and #3, the name of their neighbor across the street. Typically, people do not even know their neighbors' names. This exercise can help Christians see their neighborhoods as a mission field.

Other questions to ask: Who do we see regularly at the grocery store, dry cleaners, or favorite restaurant? Does that cashier know Jesus? What about the waitress who serves you? Ask them if there is any way you can pray for them; their answer will give you insight about their spiritual condition.

Once we allow God to give us a heart for lost people, we can begin to pray using specific strategies:

- **Prayerwalking:** One method of evangelistic prayer is prayerwalking. Praying on site will give us insight about our neighbors and their needs. In nice weather, people may be in the yard and you can engage them in conversation. If we offer to pray for our neighbors and they give a request, we then have a reason to go back to follow up with them. When neighbors know you are a praying person, they will find you in a crisis.

- **Prayer Triplets:** Prayer triplets are three friends joining in agreement to pray for three lost people each, with accountability to faithfully pray. Choose people who live near you or who you see weekly at Bible study, church, work, or in your neighborhood. Your prayer time can be as short as 15 minutes, allowing each one to lift up the three people for whom they are praying.

- **List Praying:** In preparation for an evangelistic outreach, it is a great idea to make a list of people you will commit to pray for regularly and invite to attend the event. *My Hope America* and Mission America's *LOVE2020* are both tools to encourage Christians to live a prayer-care-share lifestyle. We pray with a list, show kindness when possible, and get to know them. As God gives us the opportunity, we can share the gospel and/or show a video gospel presentation followed by our testimony and invitation.

Praying for the HEART

The goal of evangelistic praying is for the lost person's heart to be changed by the saving power of Christ. The acrostic HEART is a memory jogger. Pray for him or her to have:

- A receptive HEART (Luke 8:8,15)
- EYES that are open (Matt. 13:15; 2 Cor. 4:3–4)
- God's ATTITUDE toward sin (John 16:8)
- RELEASE to believe (2 Tim. 2:25–26)
- A TRANSFORMED life (Rom. 12:1–2).

When we understand the condition of the lost, align our hearts with God's purposes, and then actively pray for and engage those without Christ, we will experience the joy of introducing people to Jesus.

ELAINE HELMS is the director of *churchprayerministries.org* and is the author of *Prayer 101, What Every Intercessor Needs to Know*. She was the Southern Baptist prayer coordinator 2000–2010 and prayer coordinator for *My Hope America* with Billy Graham 2012–2013.

26

EFFECTIVE PRAYER
FOR THE SICK

- - - - - - - - -

By Andrew Wheeler

We pray for the sick in our churches for many reasons, such as compassion, obedience, and our desire to see God honored. But perhaps no reason is as compelling as Jesus' words: "Whatever you did for the least of these brothers and sisters of mine, you did for me" (Matt. 25:40; for context see vv. 31–46). Ministry to the sick, including prayer, is a key way to serve Jesus Himself.

Some intercessors struggle with prayer for the sick. (I'll use the term *sick* to refer to any physical or emotional impairment, short-term or long-term.) Prayer over health challenges, more than other kinds of prayer, tends to involve detailed accounts of difficulties. This can turn the focus of the prayer onto the illness and away from God.

Keys to Keeping on Target

So how can we pray effectively for the sick and mobilize this type of prayer in a church setting?

1. Keep It Vertical. "Hallowed be your name, your kingdom come" (Matt. 6:9–10).

So begins Jesus' model prayer. His prayer includes petition for physical needs (daily bread). But He begins with a vertical focus, and His focus remains vertical. This is the best framework for our prayers for the sick, too.

Later in the same chapter, Jesus urges us not to worry about life's necessities but instead focus on seeking God's Kingdom (vv. 25–34). Jesus was speaking specifically about food and clothes, but the principle applies to health as well. Health-related prayer, when it emphasizes the illness and the difficulties, can amount to spiritualized worry.

One antidote to this worry is Kingdom-focused prayer. Paul wrote to the Philippians that he expected to be set free. But his primary concern was for Christ to be exalted, whether by Paul's life or his death (Phil. 1:20). He recognized the ways God was advancing the Kingdom through his imprisonment.

2. Keep It Focused. "Your will be done" (Matt. 6:10).

We may not know God's will regarding specific healing, but we do know several things He can produce in us through trials—qualities of joy, perseverance, and maturity (James 1:2–4).

Similarly, Paul wrote to the Philippians that he had learned to be content in all circumstances (Phil. 4:11–13). Praying for the hurting person's contentment (and other growth) in the midst of their health crisis keeps us on track in praying God's will. This doesn't preclude praying specifically for healing, but it frames that prayer in a context of seeking the will of God.

3. Keep It Short. "When you pray, do not keep on babbling like pagans, for they think they will be heard because of their many words" (Matt. 6:7).

Those who came to Jesus for healing didn't recount their illnesses at length. Jesus knew leprosy, blindness, lameness, and other infirmities when He saw them. And our Father knows every detail of the illnesses we bring to Him. Not needing to recite long litanies of the difficulties frees us to focus our prayers on Him.

4. Keep It Thankful. "Do not be anxious about anything, but in every situation, by prayer and petition, with thanksgiving, present your requests to God" (Phil. 4:6).

Thankfulness is another antidote to worry. Paul's instructions tie thanksgiving to the petition, not to the answer. We can pray thankfully, knowing by faith that God hears and answers—even if we haven't seen the answer yet.

Mobilizing Prayer for the Sick

Sufferers can become consumed by their health issues, focusing their lives not on God but on their own needs. Mobilizing prayer for the sick is one way the church can share their burdens (Gal. 6:2), redirect their focus, and encourage their spiritual growth.

Here are some ways to mobilize church prayer for the sick:

1. *Small Groups.* Small groups are the best place in most churches for the practice of confession of sin and praying for healing (James 5:16). Train small group leaders to pray and lead their groups in prayer for the sick among them.
2. *Prayer Team.* Train your church's prayer team to pray for the sick.
3. *Prayer Invitations.* Set aside a regular time for prayer leaders and pastors to pray with the sick.

When we pray for the sick, we participate with God Himself in the work of intercession. The Holy Spirit intercedes with perfect wisdom beyond words (Rom. 8:26–27). Jesus Himself is also interceding along with us (Rom. 8:34; Heb. 7:25).

Let's join in!

ANDREW WHEELER served in the prayer ministry of Willow Creek Community Church for ten years and co-directed the prayer ministry at Willow Crystal Lake. He is the author of *Together in Prayer*, published by IVP.

27

A PRAYER STRATEGY FOR HUMAN TRAFFICKING

By Valerie Beck

More than 40 years ago, in a small store in northern Minnesota, a blond-haired, blue-eyed little girl stood mesmerized by trinkets in one aisle as her mother shopped in the adjacent one. Unexpectedly, a woman with a small boy told the little girl that she needed to go with them. The girl balked quietly, but she was not accustomed to opposing adults, even strangers.

From the back seat of the stranger's car, the little girl wondered how her mother would find her. By God's grace, within moments the girl's mother hurried to the parking lot and noticed her precious child in the car right next to her own. The mother jerked the door open, freed the little girl, and welcomed her back into her arms—thwarting the enemy's plans.

That little girl was me—and God did something in my life that day. Through my near abduction and other experiences, God gave me a passion for those who are taken, lured, or even given away and sold for sex.

As prayer leaders, we need to understand the reality of human trafficking—and how we can pray.

Hidden Evil

A few years ago, Minnesota hosted the Super Bowl. With any large event such as this, we can expect an increase in lewd behavior that includes purchasing women and children for sex. These hidden evils escape notice because often the transactions occur via the Internet. In Minnesota, more than 200 such ads were posted daily in the online marketplace. The profile of a "buyer" is a white, married male, age 30–50, who has disposable income and, usually, a history of pornography.

What can the Church do about all this? We offer the only true hope and healing. Jesus extends His hand to all those who are broken, lost, and living apart from Him. This includes the men who are the sellers and buyers of sex, as well as the abuse victims.

Each person is made in God's image and is valued by Him. His Word reminds us of our true enemy. His Word also reminds us that our prayers change things. As prayer leaders, we need to engage our congregations in praying about sex trafficking and sexual exploitation. Here are some ways to take action through prayer:

1. Pray that the Church
- will be willing and prepared to engage in healthy and helpful conversations about sexual exploitation, pornography, and abuse (Rom. 8:1, 5).
- will remember the gift of grace and offer prayer support and biblical truth (Eph. 2:1–9).
- will be unified and viewed as a valuable and necessary resource in this battle (John 17:23).

2. Pray that traffickers and buyers
- will find their transactions interrupted and their wicked plans frustrated (Ps. 9:16, 10:15, 146:9).
- will see the reality of what they are doing and seek help (Phil. 2:3–4; 1 Cor. 6:18–20).

3. Pray that the sold and abused

- will be found and will receive the offered help despite fear, threats, and deception (Matt. 10:28; Ps. 72:12–14).
- will experience restored minds, bodies, and lives through Christ (Zech. 9:11–12; Rom. 12:2).
- will follow through on treatment plans and learn to live in a new, healthy, and productive way (Eph. 4:22–24).
- will desire Christ alone and allow Him to fill their need for belonging, acceptance, joy, hope, and peace (Rom. 8:15; 15:13).

4. Pray that law enforcement and outreach workers

- will have a shield of physical and spiritual protection as they hear about and see the horrible violations done to the victims (Ps. 5:11–12).
- will be strengthened in Christ for the battle (Phil. 4:13).

In addition, pray that God will bring confusion into the enemy's camp so that his schemes are unorganized and ineffective (Deut. 7:23; Ps. 71:24). We desire all involved to come to repentance, to acknowledge Jesus as Lord, and to find healing and redemption in Him (2 Peter 3:9; Rom. 10:9–10).

Our God Heals

Those who are broken in body and spirit cannot be repaired without our God who heals, restores, and provides true hope for both now and eternity. What the enemy means for evil—even the horror of sex trafficking—God can turn around for His good purposes (see Gen. 50:20).

If you suspect someone is a victim or perpetrator of human trafficking, call 911 or the National Human Trafficking Hotline: 888-373-7888.

VALERIE BECK served as the outreach and justice ministries pastor at Trinity Church in Lakeville, MN.

SPECIAL INTEREST PRAYER

EMPOWERING CHRISTIAN EDUCATORS

- - - - - - - - -

By David Schmus

As the faculty adviser to my high school's Christian club years ago, I received a call from a parent who wanted to meet to pray. Like many Christian teachers in public schools, I felt isolated and alone, trying to shine my light the best I could. So I immediately agreed.

That simple after-school prayer time birthed an intercession team and a friendship that still bears fruit today.

Major Battleground

I believe the key battleground in the spiritual war for our nation is our schools. Given the extent to which our current cultural and spiritual confusion is echoed in these schools, we are seeing significant fallout:

- According to a report published in *Education Week*, between the years of 2005 and 2017, the percentage of 12- to 17-year-olds reporting a "major depressive episode" in the past year has increased from 8.7 to

13.2 percent. However, adult rates have remained constant.

- Of youth ages 12–14, three times as many girls and twice as many boys committed suicide in 2015, compared with only eight years earlier.
- At least 15 states are enabling gender confusion by allowing students to use whatever bathroom or locker room they identify with, generally without parental knowledge.

Are we losing a generation of youth to depression, suicide, and myriad other spiritual and emotional brokenness? Christian educators in our schools can be a powerful force in God's hands. However, so many educators, especially in our public schools, are fearful and isolated.

Wake Them Up

After 15 years as a public high school educator, I moved from the classroom into leadership of Christian Educators Association International. When I did so, I sensed the Lord whisper to my spirit, "My army is already in the schools. Your job is to wake them up."

But how do we help often fearful, isolated, and overworked educators to step out in faith to partner with God in bringing transformation to their classrooms and schools? You already know the answer: prayer.

As a prayer leader, you can mobilize your church to join the battle and pray in these ways:

1. Intercede for educators.

- Your local school likely has a list of faculty members on their website. Pray through the list. Send an email or note to each educator as you pray.
- Go to *everyschool.com* and sign up to pray for a specific school. Make sure your church adopts every school in your area.
- Encourage your congregation to join Moms in Prayer groups at their local schools (*momsinprayer.org*).
- Call your local schools and ask if they have a Christian club that meets there. Ask for the name of the faculty adviser. Pray for and reach out to that person.

- Don't be afraid to visit your local school, meet the principal, and ask how you can pray.

Regardless of how you target your prayers, pray that Christians in our schools will have eyes to see what God is doing on their campuses and how to partner with Him. Pray that they will not be captive to fear, but will be bold in their faith. For those in public schools, pray that they will understand what they can do legally to live out their faith. (CEAI can help with this: *ceai.org/whatwecando*.)

2. Christian educators themselves need to pray.

Administrators and teachers have a greater degree of authority to pray over their classrooms and schools. One high school principal faithfully prayerwalked his campus every morning. But when a fight broke out at his school one day, he later realized that was the only day all semester he had failed to prayerwalk.

I also know of a Christian teacher who faithfully prayed over his classroom. One of his students had been aware of a darkness that constantly followed her around at school. When she finally told this teacher and described the darkness to him, he asked, "Where is it now?"

"Oh, it's outside," she replied. "It can't come in your room."

Most Strategic

If you know Christian educators in public schools, encourage them to connect with our organization. We can protect them legally should they face opposition as they carry out their calling in their schools.

As prayer leaders, embrace these Christian educators for who they really are—possibly the most strategic missionaries in our nation.

DAVID SCHMUS is the executive director of Christian Educators Association International (*ceai.org*), which seeks to encourage, equip, and empower Christian educators to transform our public, charter, and private schools with God's love and truth.

UNIQUE PRAYER NEEDS OF THE MILITARY

- - - - - - - -

By Rebecca Shirey

During my husband's 26-year military career as an Army chaplain, I fell in love with the military lifestyle and people. I especially enjoyed the close-knit camaraderie of the on-post neighborhoods, worshiping as a community in base chapels, and the seeming ease of families to assimilate into yet another new assignment. Even with these shared bonds, the typical military family defies description. They represent a range as diverse as the U.S., but a few characteristics come to mind: resilient, mobile, adaptable, resourceful, tired.

After ten years of war on multiple fronts, the American military and their families are exhausted. Grasping the pressures of war that the military faces can be better understood if, as praying people, we apply the realities of spiritual warfare to our prayers. This will help seasoned prayer leaders guide and mobilize churches to pray more effectively for the military. Here are specific ways to pray:

1. Pray life and wholeness. The number of suicides by service members in 2012 outnumbered the troops lost in combat that year. Despite many programs to stem this trend, the numbers remain almost the same so far this year. Programs aren't the answer.

John tells us, "The thief comes only to steal and kill and destroy; I have come that they may have life, and have it to the full" (10:10). At-risk members of the military need to grasp this promise of abundant life made possible through Jesus Christ! But not every hurting person considers suicide. Many returning service members provide examples of courage and faith. Pray for their strength and continued healing.

2. Pray for re-integration into civilian life. It's easy to see how multiple deployments can take their toll, but re-integration can be just as challenging. With the drawdown of the war and the decreasing numbers of U.S. forces, the civilian workforce must now accommodate service members returning home.

Pray for increased opportunities and financial peace. Financial issues remain a leading cause of family breakdown.

3. Pray for healed families. Long separations present challenges to the husband or wife serving, as well as the family remaining behind. Physical and emotional wounds, death, divorce, and disappointments cause havoc in any marriage and family. These realities face many military families. Pray for the chaplains serving as marriage and family counselors. Pray for wisdom to speak hope into tough situations.

My husband Lou and I recently conducted breakout sessions at Ancora, a training event at the Army War College in Carlisle, PA. One keynote presenter recounted how she was left with four children to raise after losing her husband in an explosion in Iraq. She said, "The bomb went off in Iraq, but the shrapnel hit our home."

This family now models the hope and healing possible through faith in Jesus. Pray that many more will be able to testify to God's grace.

4. Pray for religious freedom of expression. Attempts to restrain religious expression, especially Christian witness, are not challenges limited to the military. It is a reflection of the climate of our country. Contrary to what many believe, within chapel settings, Jesus is proclaimed. Chaplains are required to uphold all the teaching and beliefs of their endorsing denominations. Many military bases have vibrant religious programs and outreaches.

Nevertheless, financial constraints and political concerns have hampered and eliminated strong programs uniting families and growing disciples of Jesus. Pray for wisdom and favor as chaplains navigate these new policies.

5. Pray for revival. The military brings together people from multi-denominational backgrounds. Imagine how a move of God throughout the military community could quickly spread to denominations throughout the United States.

The military is a forerunner in many areas. They led the way in integration with the Tuskegee Airmen. They were among the first to include women in the workforce. Many medical advances came as a result of urgent needs on the battlefield.

The military can also be a forerunner in a great awakening. The challenges facing military personnel create fertile ground for revival.

6. Pray for victory over difficult circumstances. When King Jehoshaphat and the Israelites faced terrorizing threats from an enemy, the people cried out to the Lord. He heard their prayers, bringing them an encouraging message through a prophet. "This is what the Lord says to you: 'Do not be afraid or discouraged because of this vast army. For the battle is not yours, but God's'" (2 Chron. 20:15).

The vast issues facing the military today present no challenge for God. Pray for God's intervention as war comes home. And pray that He will be glorified in the midst of the challenges.

REBECCA SHIREY travels internationally as a speaker at conferences and retreats. She served as an advisor from 2006–2010 for Protestant Women of the Chapel International. She and her husband Lou served the denominational prayer ministry of the International Pentecostal Holiness Church.

30

ASSISTING YOUR CHURCH IN PRAYING FOR ISRAEL

By Dale Schlafer

A local prayer leader emailed me about how she might assist her congregation in praying for Israel. This is my response to her, acknowledging that mobilizing others to pray for Israel requires understanding of biblical prophecy, theological differences, and wisdom from the Lord:

Dear Suzan,

Thank you for your recent email asking how you, as a local prayer leader, might be able to generate prayer for Israel within your local congregation.

Christians in America tend to be poorly educated regarding the place of Israel in the Bible and what is taking place in the nation of Israel today. This ignorance stems largely from the media in this country who have essentially hijacked public opinion. Seek wisdom from the Lord as you search for accurate sources of information to bring both the truth of Israel's place in the Word and current events to your congregation.

Direct news from Israel is a good place to start. Contact *newsletter@*

timesofisrael.com for *The Times of Israel* daily edition or *jpost.com* for the *Jerusalem Post*.

As you begin educating your congregation, it is important to note that there tends to be a wide divide between millennials and older generations. The younger generation may look at Israel as an occupier who has no right to be in the land known as Israel. This position can be largely attributed to a biased media portrayal that is hostile to Israel.

Older folks likely were raised to see the return of Israel as fulfilling biblical prophecy. Trust that as you lead your congregation to the passages in Scripture to pray (Gen. 12–13, 15; Zech. 14; Rom. 11), millennials will come to see the truth of God's Word, and the older generations will be reenergized with a forgotten truth.

One of your most difficult tasks will be to bring both Jewish and Arab followers of Jesus Christ before your congregation. Both of these groups face enormous pressures from the nation of Israel and their respective cultures. Keep in mind that 75 percent of the nation of Israel does not follow any religious faith, but does identify as Jewish by birth. Out of a population of 8 million, only about 20,000 are serious followers of Christ. This number is broken down roughly into 15,000 Messianic Jews and 5,000 Arabs. There may be as many as 140,000 Arabs identified as Christians; however, only about 5,000 claim a commitment to Christ.

In addition to cultural pressures, theological differences between Messianic and Arab believers regarding the actual land of Israel present huge hurdles to these groups moving together in unity. In order to help identify specific issues for prayer, contact *arrowsfromzion@gmail.com* to subscribe to the weekly compilation of primarily Messianic ministries. It will provide insight into many congregations and ministries in Israel.

Second, check out *hope-nazareth.org*, which is a ministry led by a dynamic Arab woman who is deeply committed to the "one new man" (Eph. 2:15, Col. 3:10).

Peace of Jerusalem

In addition, Suzan, something that has really changed my life in recent years is praying for Messianic and Arab believers by name. In previous years, I followed biblical instruction and prayed "for the peace of Jerusalem" (Ps. 122:6). However, I had little emotional investment. This changed when I began praying for specific individuals, congregations, and issues. I encourage your congregation to adopt both a Messianic and an Arab congregation to help make this emotional connection as well as to illustrate the "one new man" which Christ came to create.

You asked about establishing some kind of rhythm in praying for Israel. "Rhythm" is actually an excellent choice of words. I would recommend you consider something I have found helpful—focusing corporate prayer around the timing of the three feasts God commanded Israel to celebrate each year: Passover, Shavot (Pentecost), and Succoth (Tabernacles/Booths).

Following the pattern of these feasts provides nice symmetry. Passover is always close to our Resurrection celebration, Pentecost is 50 days after that, and Tabernacles is always in the fall. By doing corporate prayer on or around these feasts, you have the opportunity to teach your congregation about the feasts as you lead them in praying for Israel.

Suzan, if you should get flack for making Israel an emphasis of prayer, refer those folks to Genesis 12:3, where God says: "I will bless those who bless you [speaking to Abraham, the father of the Jews] and whoever curses you I will curse."

Why pray for Israel? Because we want them—and us—to receive God's blessing. Every blessing to you as you undertake this biblical call from the Lord.

Your brother, Dale

DALE SCHLAFER is the co-founder and president of the Center for World Revival and Awakening (*revivalandawakening.org*). He and his wife Liz spent four months a year in Israel, ministering with the Ecclesia (Church) there.

This handbook is a compilation of "Prayer Leader" columns from *Prayer Connect* magazine. To subscribe to the magazine or become a member of The Church Prayer Leaders Network (CPLN), go to *prayerleader.com*. As a member of CPLN, you will have access to more than 700 ideas, articles and training videos to help you grow as a catalyst and leader for prayer in your church.

CAROL MADISON is the founding editor of *Prayer Connect* magazine and a member of America's National Prayer Committee. She also directs the prayer ministries at Hillside Church of Bloomington, MN, and is the author of *Prayer That's Caught and Taught: Mentoring the Next Generation*, available from *prayershop.org*.

Do you want to see a greater passion for prayer in your church?

Are you equipped to be a catalyst for prayer in your congregation?

Then you need to be a member of the

The Church Prayer Leaders Network exists to encourage, challenge, inspire, and resource you as you seek to motivate and mobilize your church toward deeper levels of prayer.

Benefits of Membership:
- Annual subscription to *Prayer Connect* magazine
- Receive "Prayer Leader Online," a bi-monthly email that includes suggestions, inspiration and resource ideas to help you in your ministry of developing prayer.
- Discounts on prayer resources at prayershop.org

Go to prayerleader.com/membership or call 812 238-5504 to join.